The Gaelic World at War: Soldiers & Soldiering in Ireland 1366–1547

Fergus Cannan-Braniff

Helion & Company Limited
Unit 8 Amherst Business Centre
Budbrooke Road
Warwick
CV34 5WE
England
Tel. 01926 499 619
Email: info@helion.co.uk
Website: www.helion.co.uk
X (formerly Twitter): @helionbooks
Facebook: @HelionBooks
Visit our blog https://helionbooks.wordpress.com/

Published by Helion & Company 2025
Designed and typeset by Mary Woolley, Battlefield Design (www.battlefield-design.co.uk)
Cover designed by Paul Hewitt, Battlefield Design (www.battlefield-design.co.uk)

Text ©Fergus Cannan-Braniff 2025
Illustrations © as individually credited
Colour artwork drawn by Seán Ó Brógain © Helion & Company 2025
Maps drawn by Anderson Subtil © Helion & Company 2025

Every reasonable effort has been made to trace copyright holders and to obtain their permission for the use of copyright material. The author and publisher apologise for any errors or omissions in this work and would be grateful if notified of any corrections that should be incorporated in future reprints or editions of this book.

ISBN 978-1-804518-32-8

British Library Cataloguing-in-Publication Data.
A catalogue record for this book is available from the British Library.

All rights reserved. No part of this publication may be reproduced, stored in a retrieval system, or transmitted, in any form, or by any means, electronic, mechanical, photocopying, recording or otherwise, without the express written consent of Helion & Company Limited.

For details of other military history titles published by Helion & Company Limited contact the above address or visit our website: http://www.helion.co.uk.

We always welcome receiving book proposals from prospective authors.

Dedication

This book is dedicated to my daughter Matilda and my son Patrick

Contents

Acknowledgements		vii
Abbreviations		viii
Prologue: Groundworks in Medieval Gaelic Military History		ix
1	Ceithearnach: Ireland's 'Ordinary Soldier' Reimagined	15
2	Gallóglach: Perspectives on the Axeman	40
3	Body Size & Fitness as a Part of Gaelic Military Selection	63
4	'Natives'? 'Auxiliaries'? The Social & Cultural Character of Kern	79
5	Out of the Shadows: Reconstructing the Daltinne & Gairm Shluaigh Fighter	87
6	Redshanks as Marines	94
7	Marcshlua: The 'Knights' of A Gaelic Army	99
8	Marshals & Constables: European Trends in Ireland	104
9	The Collapse of the Gaelic Recovery	109
Colour Plate Commentaries		111
Bibliography		119

Acknowledgements

For their help, discussions and knowledge, I would like to thank Peter Basham, Cormac Bourke, Myles Campbell, Dr Freddie Hulbert, Fergus Gillespie, Dr Jim Higgins, Ian Kelso, Roy King, Hon. Hector McDonnell, the late Bob Paisley, Patrick Smethurst, Prof. Brendan Smith, Graham Nisbet, Dr Calum Robertson, C. L. Stopford Sackville, Peter Ubly, and my mother Cresone Cannan. I would also like to thank the staff at the Royal Collections, Heathfield Library, National Museum of Ireland and Trinity College Dublin. I would particularly like to thank Russell Moore for discussing so many of the themes which appear in this book. My thanks as well to Charles Singleton and Stephen Ede-Borrett at Helion. And, as always, my gratitude and love to my wife Heather.

Abbreviations

Carew: Carew Manuscripts in Lambeth Palace Library
DIB: *Dictionary of Irish Biography*
IE TCD: Manuscripts in Trinity College Dublin
NA: National Archives, London
OCIH: *The Oxford Companion to Irish History*
ODNB: *Oxford Dictionary of National Biography*
OED: *Complete Oxford English Dictionary*
RIA: Manuscripts in Royal Irish Academy

Prologue

Groundworks in Medieval Gaelic Military History

> …if they make any mention of Ireland, they either heap hearsay and lies on it through ignorance, or they stab at it with distressing abuse through impudence.
>
> Richard Stanihurst describing in his book, *Great Deeds in Ireland* (published 1584), the attitude of scholars to Ireland.

London at the height of the Victorian age. A woman visits the British Museum's print room wanting to draw a picture of Irish warriors. We do not know her name, but the artist who made the picture she hopes to copy was Albrecht Dürer.

Dürer's original is in Berlin but staff at the British Museum produce a copy in their print room for the visiting artist to work from. The staff, however, are unsure which of the figures in Dürer's image is a 'galloglass' or Gaelic heavy infantryman, which is a problem as the woman has said she would make a drawing of an authentic 'Irish galloglass' for William Hugh Patterson, an eminent enthusiast for all things relating to Ireland's past.[1]

Patterson, from Strandtown near Belfast, had been working in his father's ironmongery business since he was 16, but had managed to find the time to make a name for himself in circles concerned with geology, fossils, archaeology, history, animal welfare and the Ulster dialect.[2] In a letter of 27 October 1871 Patterson told another distinguished amateur antiquary, the Rev. James Graves, that he was working on a 'paper on the Galloglass slab' – a reference to an evocative tomb at Killybegs, Donegal, depicting what must

---

1 RIA MS 24 O 39/JG/11a.
2 'Patterson, Sir Robert Lloyd,' *DIB* (entry by P. M. Byrne); 'Graves, James,' *DIB* (entry by F. C. Williams).

THE GAELIC WORLD AT WAR: SOLDIERS & SOLDIERING IN IRELAND 1366–1547

Gold ring brooch, with a diameter of 29mm, found in the ruins of the Franciscan Friary at Enniscorthy, Co. Wexford, in the collection of the British Museum. (Drawing by Heather Cannan-Braniff)

surely be a member of the famous MacSweeney or Mac Suibhne family of galloglass clutching an axe.[3] Patterson says in the same letter that his female friend (he does not name her) 'undertook to make a copy of the etching by albert Dürer in the British Museum,' but that she 'had considerable difficulty in finding out who the proper figure to copy' was.[4] Patterson adds that the 'authorities in the print room took some trouble in trying to find my friend what she wanted, but were not able to point out any one figure in particular, as being an Irish galloglass' before eventually they 'supposed that one these might be the figure she wanted.'[5] After consulting with Patterson by letter, she then made an accomplished drawing of one of Dürer's warriors, 'but she does not know, nor do the museum people, what it represents.'[6]

The Weaknesses of Gaelic Military History

It is no surprise that Dürer's image of Irish warriors caught the imagination of Patterson and his artist friend. Being fascinated by the image, debating and discussing it, is something of a rite of passage for anyone with an interest in Gaelic military history. Dürer's ink and water colour picture, initialled and dated 1521, probably brings to life Gaelic soldiers of the period more vividly than any other medieval or renaissance image.

Dürer's achievement in this image is that he succeeds in showing us apparently real people. And yet the military history of the Gaelic nations – Ireland, Scotland and also the Isle of Man – has been a blind spot for historians. The simple truth is that most historians are not very interested in Gaelic military history, the subject being regarded as unimportant, 'fringe' and the preserve of cranks and eccentrics. Interestingly, re-enactors and model-makers – regardless of their nationality – have often shown much more interest in the Gaelic soldiers of the past than the academics. Granted, progress has been made in deciphering the terminology of Irish military obligation and tribute ('coyne and livery', for example).[7] But it was human beings and horses that decided events at battles such as Clontarf and Knockdoe, not terminology. The military history of medieval Ireland

---

3   RIA MS 24 O 39/JG/11a.
4   RIA MS 24 O 39/JG/11a.
5   RIA MS 24 O 39/JG/11a.
6   RIA MS 24 O 39/JG/11a. The drawing was sent with the letter and is catalogued under the same RIA reference.
7   See the excellent glossary in K. Simms, *From Kings to Warlords: The Changing Political Structure of Gaelic Ireland in the Later Middle Ages* (Woodbridge: Boydell Press, 1987).

has become oddly depopulated, and we need to bring back to the fore the people and animals who did the hard work.

The problem is that traditionally historians have regarded medieval Irish and Scottish soldiers as 'wild', 'primitive', 'backward' and 'cruel'. When historians do speak of Gaelic soldiers, it is in hyperbole. A new wave of military history may have ditched the notion that European medieval warfare was nothing but ill-disciplined clashes of reckless knights,[8] but Scotland and Ireland are denied space in this revised picture because, allegedly, the Gaelic nations were a 'Celtic fringe' beyond the European cultural 'mainstream', meaning they lacked a 'knightly' or 'chivalrous' code of soldierly conduct.

But from the available evidence it does not appear that medieval Gaelic soldiers were especially backward or quixotic. Nearly 30 years ago Marie Therese Flanagan remarked that negative perceptions of the skill and equipment of early medieval Irish soldiers are driven more by 'assumption' than 'detailed studies'.[9] Sadly, this is still true, for both the earlier and the later Middle Ages. In truth, some of the myths are so flimsy we can knock them down now. Relying on very wobbly caricatures of hot-headed Celts, the claim is often made, for instance, that Irish Gaels were unable to take castles. Castles were rarely easy to take in medieval Europe, but the records suggest the inability of Irish armies to take castles has been exaggerated. It was said that Laighseach Ó Mórdha, an Irish chief who died in 1342, burnt eight English-held castles in one evening, and destroyed the Mortimer stronghold at Dunamase.[10] Likewise, Ó Néill forces were able to spend six months from the autumn of 1470 to the spring of 1471 taking the castle of Omagh.[11]

Top of the list, though, is the old myth that, in the words of the famous military historian Sir Charles Oman, Gaelic Irish soldiers were good skirmishers but 'easily' routed in open terrain.[12] But were the results always so disastrous on the battlefield? Gaelic Irish armies were able to win battles (sometimes small in scale) against English soldiers and their allies in Louth in 1346, Ulster in 1374, probably again the same year in Antrim, in Co. Kilkenny in 1386, north Co. Carlow in 1398, and against forces sent out from the English Pale in 1423, somewhere probably north-east of Meath.[13]

---

8   S. McLynn gave a very good introduction to these issues in 'The Myths of Medieval Warfare' in *History Today*, 44, no. 1 (1994).
9   M. T. Flanagan, 'Irish and Anglo-Norman Warfare in Twelfth Century Ireland' in T. Bartlett & K. Jeffery (eds.), *A Military History of Ireland* (Cambridge: Cambridge University Press, 1996), p.52.
10 D. McGettigan, *Richard II and the Irish Kings* (Dublin: Four Courts Press, 2016), p.50.
11 Simms, *Kings to Warlords*, p.127.
12 Charles Oman, *History of the Art of War in the Middle Ages* (Oxford: Blackwell, 1885. Uckfield: Naval & Military Press reprint), vol. 1, p.404.
13 McGettigan, *Richard II*, pp.100, 127–128 & 163; 'Warfare,' *OCIH* (entry by K. Simms); F. Cannan, *Galloglass 1250–1600: Gaelic Mercenary Warrior* (Oxford:

THE GAELIC WORLD AT WAR: SOLDIERS & SOLDIERING IN IRELAND 1366–1547

If you say these were mere skirmishes or raids, we should clarify that some Gaelic raids were major operations. When Art Mór Mac Murchadha (or MacMurrough) attacked and burnt the English settlement at Carlow in 1378 he did so with a reported 2,000 horse and foot.[14] There was no clear line between battle, skirmish and raid; a single engagement could involve all three. More importantly, the accusation that (again quoting Oman) Irish soldiers were 'unable to stand firm,'[15] feels instinctively wrong when one remembers those battles in which Irish soldiers (not necessarily all of them) stood firm: Clontarf (1014), Dysert O'Dea (1318), Piltown (1462, involving perhaps 5,000 warriors), Knockdoe (1504, involving perhaps as many as 10,000 warriors), or later battles (still fought with late medieval Gaelic troop types) such as Affane (1565), Farsetmore (1567) and Shrule (1570) – and the list goes on.[16]

It must also say something positive about the quality of Irish soldiers that they were considered worthy of recruitment by the English for attacks on Scotland and France: Irish soldiers served 'in most, if not all, the early Anglo-Norman field armies,'[17] and almost 3,500 Irish troops, to give a later example, served in England's 1303–1304 Scottish campaign.[18] Nor does it not take long to find examples of Gaelic armies performing tactical movements, not just crazed charges, that would have required both skill and a cool head. For example, in 1434 disaster was averted thanks to a daring intervention from Mac Suibhne galloglasses who rescued their chief's army from the English.[19] Yet historians cling to the idea that the galloglass's only metier was the mêlée. The truth is that they *were* excellent in the muddled fury of the mêlée, but they patently also had the skills to perform more complex, considered actions.

Furthermore, there is evidence showing Gaelic soldiers were fit and hardy, not through genetic accident but as a result of training. Training is likewise the only plausible explanation for the high level of

Shoe, probably late fifteenth century, found in Kilcummin, Co. Offaly. (© National Museum of Ireland)

Osprey, 2010), pp.40–41; 'Mac Suibhne Fánad' in F. Gillespie, 'The Gaelic Families of Donegal,' in W. Nolan, L. Ronayne & M. Dunlevy (eds.), *Donegal: History and Society* (Dublin: Geography Publications, 1995).

14 McGettigan, *Richard II*, p.100.
15 Oman, *History*, vol. 1, p.403.
16 The figure of approx. 10,000 at Knockdoe is G. A. Hayes-McCoy's estimate: *Irish Battles: A Military History of Ireland* (Belfast: Appletree Press, 1990), pp.53 & 61–62. The approx. 5,000 at Piltown is from T. O'Neill, 'Edmund MacRichard Butler: Books and Warfare in Fifteenth-Century Ireland' in *History Ireland*, vol. 23 (July/August 2015).
17 Flanagan, 'Irish and Anglo-Norman Warfare' in Bartlett & Jeffery, *Military History of Ireland*, p.67.
18 'Wogan, Sir John,' *ODNB* (entry by G. J. Hand).
19 'Mac Suibhne Fánad,' in Gillespie, 'Gaelic Families of Donegal' in Nolan, Ronayne & Dunlevy, *Donegal*.

combat skill among Gaelic soldiers. How else can we explain the bouts of single combat in which Gaelic soldiers beat high-status Anglo-Irish or English soldiers (who appear to be themselves well trained)? In 1392 Niall Óg Ó Néill, ruler of Tyrone, killed Geoffrey (Seifin) White, keeper of the peace for Co. Louth, in single combat; Niall possibly killed a second English nobleman on the same occasion.[20] It was claimed, too, that at the 1423 Meath engagement a Mac Suibhne galloglass slew an important English knight.[21] These are not soldiers relying solely on instinct and bloodlust: these are military professionals who have undergone thorough training.

Time Frame and Line of Argument

Put simply, the purpose of this book is to clear away the maligning myths surrounding late medieval Gaelic soldiers, and to at last give them a fair hearing. This book does not argue that Gaelic armies were invincible or that they were better than the English, or even that they were as good as English armies. Rather, this book merely invites the reader to consider the following possibilities:

1. That late medieval Gaelic armies, both Irish and Scottish, should not be regarded as bands of mindless thugs, but as something more organised and professional than that.
2. That Gaelic armies were neither especially antiquated nor utterly different to the armies raised in the rest of medieval Europe.
3. That common sense makes it hard to accept the view that Gaelic soldiers were so unremittingly stupid or conservative as to fight for centuries in ineffective ways.
4. That late medieval Gaelic military systems of hierarchy, organisation and training have similarities with those of other European nations.
5. That historians should express their thoughts in more cautious language and recognise the contestability and uncertainty of much of history – particularly when it comes to dating objects and describing what they think those objects 'show' about Gaelic history.
6. That Irish military reform and the sharing of military theory was not something that began with the 'military revolution.'

The book spans, roughly, the period from the Statutes of Kilkenny of 1366 until the death of Henry VIII in 1547. This is not to claim that one

---

20   McGettigan, *Richard II*, p.137.
21   Cannan, *Galloglass*, p.40.

THE GAELIC WORLD AT WAR: SOLDIERS & SOLDIERING IN IRELAND 1366-1547

world began in 1366 and another ended in 1547. Largely unenforceable, the Kilkenny statutes are nonetheless an arresting statement of the English government's opinions about what 'Englishness' was, and what, in their opinion, needed to be done in Ireland. The Kilkenny statutes were passed during a period historians call the 'Gaelic recovery,' when English control of Ireland (or at least, of non-urban Ireland) was weak. With huge areas of Ireland left unconquered and unruled by England, an Irish soldier alive in 1366 may well have felt optimistic about the future.[22] With hindsight, Ireland in the fourteenth, fifteenth and early sixteenth centuries was something of a golden age for high quality individual soldiering. The armies of the Gaelic recovery era were not characterised by nostalgia or seeking a return to a misty Gaeldom of standing stones and arcane tradition, but were bold and forward looking, incorporating new ideas while preserving the best of the old.

Arms of Mac Suibhne or MacSweeney in a herald's manuscript in the National Library of Ireland. (Image courtesy of Fergus Gillespie)

An Irish soldier in 1547 – by which time Henry VIII had granted himself the title of King of Ireland and brought about the reformation – may well have felt more uneasy about the future. The years that followed were of Gaelic political and military decline; the Gaelic recovery was over. Yet history is not neat, and many of the sources quoted here come from after 1547, since many old military practices survived in Ireland, and even more so Scotland, long after the end mid-1500s – not only out of respect for the old ways, but because many of those old ways continued to deliver the goods.

Viewed, then, in the context of so much misleading historiography, the uncertainty of the British Museum staff, Patterson and the female artist as to which of the figures was a galloglass is, rather than a frustration, a very healthy starting point for a reappraisal of late medieval Irish soldiers and soldiering.

---

22 An excellent map of Ireland *c.* 1350 in *OCIH* shows the extent of English conquest and political control.

1

Ceithearnach: Ireland's 'Ordinary Soldier' Reimagined

To distress the enemy more by famine than the sword is a mark of consummate skill.

Vegetius

Echoing a Hebrew proverb that 'Soldiers fight, and kings are heroes' was the eighteenth century saying, 'It is the common soldier's blood that makes the general a great man.'[1] If you play chess in Ireland you may have heard a pawn referred to as a 'kern,' and the real life flesh-and-blood kern was indeed the pawn or ordinary professional soldier of Irish armies from the High Middle Ages down into the period of Oliver Cromwell and perhaps even beyond.[2] Steven Ellis has calculated that of the 22,000 or so Irish soldiers in a report made towards the close of the fifteenth century, over 70 percent were kern.[3] Though Richard Stanihurst defined the 'kerne' for Raphael Holinshed's *Chronicles* (first published 1577) as 'an ordinary souldior,' they have received almost no attention from historians.[4] When they have it has been to condemn them as badly equipped savages useless for anything other than brawls and torching property.

---

1   R. Palmer (ed.), *The Rambling Soldier* (Gloucester: Alan Sutton, 1985), p.1.
2   *Concise English-Irish Dictionary: Foclóir Béarla-Gaeilge*, chief ed. P. Ó Mianáin (Dublin, 2021), 'pawn,' p.1067; F. Cannan, 'Generation of Villains,' *Military Illustrated*, no. 275 (April 2011), p.31.
3   S. G. Ellis, *Ireland in the Age of the Tudors 1447–1603: English Expansion and the End of Gaelic Rule* (Abingdon: Routledge, 2014), p.249.
4   Richard Stanihurst (L. Miller & E. Power eds) *Holinshed's Irish Chronicle*, (Dublin: Dolmen, 1979), p.114; Raphael Holinshed, *Chronicles*, (London, 1587, 2nd edn), volume 2, p.45.

THE GAELIC WORLD AT WAR: SOLDIERS & SOLDIERING IN IRELAND 1366-1547

Adopted into the English language in the 1300s or 1400s, 'kern' is an anglicising of a much older Irish word *ceithearnach* (singular), from the Irish plural *ceithearn* for 'war-band' or 'troop.' The word 'kern' came to have a colourful array of meanings in early modern English literature, including an Irish rebel, yokel or bandit.[5] Sometimes Tudor writers slapped the word kern on any Irish foot soldier (including galloglass), and this careless use of the word persists among the academic community today. Although kern does not literally mean much more than trooper, it clearly meant to the more careful writers and record-keepers an Irish light infantryman, or as A. L. Rowse (who was very negative about the Gaelic Irish) put it: 'the light (very light) infantry' of Gaelic Ireland.[6]

Some modern historians use the word 'kern' to describe the mass of lightly-armed tenant farmers and peasants called up during wartime in the *gairm shluaigh* or traditional Gaelic muster of a chief's able-bodied adult males.[7] Others, however, restrict the use of the word to the professional light infantry retained by the chiefs.[8] The answer is that, strictly speaking, a kern was a member of a professional *ceithearn*, or war-band, and not a local man answering his chief's call to arms.

Be that as it may, aspects of the kern hark back to the local levy, which created the template for the kern as a lightly-armed infantryman since that is how, out of poverty and lack of resources, most of the people answering the local muster were probably equipped. Light infantry were moreover useful in the rugged, watery Irish countryside, and presumably Irish chiefs got used to thinking of skirmisher-scouts as the normal, standard type of fighting man they needed for their armies. To look at, the kern may often have appeared something of a replica of the communal peasant militia – but a replica who had been professionalised, was paid for his services and had the time to hone his skills.

Many *ceithearnaigh* (plural), were itinerant soldiers for hire – but not all of them. In the fifteenth and sixteenth centuries there were groups of kern called *ceithearn tighe* or 'household troops,' in other words soldiers retained more or less permanently in one chief's household. In 1468, for instance, 'sixty retained kerns' were serving a Burke nobleman.[9] As so often with medieval terminology, the term was used loosely, and to late medieval and Tudor ears kern was a catch-all term for any Irish light infantryman, whether a full-time household guardsman, a wandering mercenary, a man

---

5 F. Cannan, 'Hags of Hell: Late Medieval Irish Kern,' *History Ireland*, volume 19, no. 1 (January/February 2011), pp.15–16; K. Simms, *Gaelic Ulster in the Middle Ages: History, Culture and Society* (Dublin: Four Courts Press: 2020), p.412.
6 A. L. Rowse, *The Expansion of Elizabethan England* (London: Macmillan, 1971), p.113.
7 For instance, G. A. Hayes-McCoy, *Scots Mercenary Forces in Ireland (1567–1603)* (Dublin: Edmund Burke, 1996), p.359.
8 For instance, K. Simms, 'Kern,' *OCIH*.
9 J. O'Donovan (trans. and ed.), *Annals of the Kingdom of Ireland, by the Four Masters* (Dublin: 1856, 2nd edn), volume 4, p.1057.

CEITHEARNACH: IRELAND'S 'ORDINARY SOLDIER' REIMAGINED

Map showing the lands of some of Ireland's most powerful families. (Author's artwork)

hired for a specific campaign, a peasant conscript or an individual involved in a revolt – so long as the individual in question fought on foot and was lightly equipped.

The English use of the word kern to mean a peasant or rural troublemaker probably offers a fairly accurate glimpse of the origins of many rank-and-file kern, who appear to have been a mix of locally recruited rural 'heavies', possibly some of them younger sons of minor noble families, and what were called 'idle men' (perhaps unemployed soldiers, unemployed farm workers and criminals). This is much the same line-up of men one would have found in a medieval English free company, or any other European mercenary infantry unit. Many kern were probably of a much less respectable type than the husbandmen and peasants called up in the *gairm shluaigh*.

Mainly Gaelic Irishmen, there were also Gaelicised Anglo-Irish kern. Some kern officers (Keatings, Purcells and probably Archdeacons) came from landed families, and one imagines these country gentry recruited many of the rank-and-file kern from whatever 'idle men' and adventurers they could dredge out of their lands. Although being a warrior was a sign of status in Gaelic society, kern were ranked in precedence below galloglass, who in turn came below horsemen, by late sixteenth and early seventeenth century writers.[10] Kern wages were correspondingly modest: the accounts of the justiciar Ralph Ufford, who died in 1346, record that kern were paid 1d a day, whereas archers received 2d a day.[11]

Historians call kern and galloglass 'mercenaries' but the word does not entirely do them justice since

Portrait in black and red ink and watercolour by Hans Holbein the Younger of James Butler, 9th Earl of Ormond, who was born around 1496, and was in England August 1537 to August 1538 (when, presumably, he sat for Holbein). If the identification is correct this is one the earliest known naturalistic portraits of an Irish noble, the man in Holbein's portrait certainly looks the part. Holbein portrays a well-fed lord with a ginger beard who looks like he has never gone hungry in his life, and who looks like he would have the stately presence to have a *craic* with his galloglass and kern (of whom James Butler had many) and hold the respect of his followers. (© Royal Collection Enterprises Limited 2025 / Royal Collection Trust)

---

10 Holinshed, *Chronicles*, volume 2, p.45; Richard Stanihurst (J. Barry & H. Morgan, trans. & ed.), *Great Deeds in Ireland* (Togher: Cork University Press, 2015), pp.123–1255; Barnabe Rich, *A New Description of Ireland* (London: Thomas Adams, 1610), p.37; John Dymmok, *A Treatice of Ireland* (Dublin: Irish Archaeological Society, 1842), p.7.
11 Simms, 'Kern,' *OCIH*.

they were often very loyal, had a respect for Gaelic customs and traditions, and serving the English interest in Ireland (which they sometimes did) does not ever appear to have been their long-term goal. Kern and galloglass were decidedly Gaelic in their political and cultural alignments, and we should instead think of them as part of Gaelic Ireland's professional warrior class rather than straightforwardly ruthless soldiers of fortune.[12]

Even if they had been outlaws, brigands or vagrants, one assumes a sensible chief would only select kern who were loyal and disciplined enough to follow orders. Irish armies must have varied a great deal across different parts of the country depending on the region's wealth, and how much of a priority defence was to the region's rulers. Indeed, the advanced reenactor or modelmaker should go beyond generic portrayals of 'Irish' soldiers and give thought to what part of Ireland they are representing.

No doubt some chiefs fielded ill-disciplined rabbles, but the best Irish armies were clearly not like this. It was reported that, far from being an unmanageable mob, the army of Piers Butler, 8th Earl of Ormond (died 1539), would only take its orders from the Earl himself or his son, James, the future 9th Earl.[13] It is a cliché to think of Irish warriors as anarchic tempestuous rascals prone to back-stabbing – some kern, however, were extremely loyal. Gerald Fitzgerald, 14th or 15th (depending on your

The fact that the Irish could erect an impressive stone structure such as the Grianán of Aileach in Donegal, during the sixth or seventh century suggests it was not ignorance that prevented them from building castles in stone, which they started in earnest in the later 1300s. (Artwork by F. Cannan-Braniff)

12 See 'F. Cannan, 'Machiavellian Mercenaries? Galloglass Scruples of Politics, Culture & Religion' (published on the Helion website, 2025).

13 'Butler [Bocach], James, Ninth Earl of Ormond and Second Earl of Ossory,' *ODNB* (entry by D. Edwards). Even if they did vary in quality, few medieval kern can have been as hopeless as the early modern retainers employed by the 1st Duke of Ormond. When Ormond was attacked in 1670 by Thomas Blood and others, Ormond's retainers simply ran away. Blood would have got a very different reception if he had tried to jump a medieval Ormond and his kern! See R. Hutchinson, *The Audacious Crimes of Colonel Blood* (London: Weidenfeld & Nicolson, 2016), chap. 5.

numbering system) Earl of Desmond, began his war with Elizabeth I with an army; his war ended with a band of followers comprising one kern, two horsemen, a chaplain and a boy.[14] If only we could ask that kern and boy why they stayed with Desmond when so many more powerful people had deserted him…

As well as fierce and bellicose, kern were able skirmishers and scouts, and we should imagine a competent kern as an individual who is vigilant, alert and attuned to their surroundings, enabling them to monitor travel in and out of their chief's territory. Kern were not just fighters; in addition to guarding the chief, they were also used to enforce local law and order, 'Kearne' being defined in a 1587 glossary of rents and customs which had been due to the Earl of Desmond as 'soldiers [who] aide & assist the Justices, seneshalls, receavors, stewardes of courtes, & serjeantes.'[15] It is important to remember that, however violent and parasitical Gaelic soldiers could be, there was no other source of law and order available.

Limited Combat Value?

Historians are generally very negative about the kerns' military effectiveness. But accounts from people who had actually fought the Irish tell a different story. Kern were still part of warfare when Thomas Gainsford, an English writer and officer, served in Ireland at the start of the seventeenth century. In short, Gainsford does not say kern were useless, instead, he says 'Kern' were 'excellent' skirmishers and 'sufficient souldiers' (probably meaning battlefield work).[16] If we have understood Gainsford correctly, he is saying that kern were not first-rate as line infantry, but they were acceptable. Gainsford adds that kern were still 'in great reputation' in the 1600s, unlike the galloglass who had passed into history.[17] Jean Froissart, a chronicler who lived during the Hundred Years' War, wrote an account of Richard II's 1394–1395 campaign in Ireland based on the experiences of an Englishman who was there, in which the Irish (most of whom would have been kern) are described not as hopeless brutes, but as 'skilled fighters.'[18]

Certainly, the Achilles' heel of Irish armies was that kern were fielded as if they were suitable for the line of battle, when in fact their way of fighting was that of a specialist light infantry. It is unclear what happened at the Battle of Stoke Field in 1487, but it is claimed Irish troops (possibly

---

14 'Fitzgerald, Gerald FitzJames, Fourteenth Earl of Desmond,' *ODNB* (entry by J. J. N. McGurk).
15 H. F. Hore & J. Graves (eds.), *The Social State of the Southern and Eastern Counties of Ireland in the 16th Century* (Dublin: Kilkenny and South East Ireland Archaeological Society, 1870), p.266.
16 Thomas Gainsford, *The Glory of England* (London, 1620, 2nd edn), p.149.
17 Gainsford, *Glory of England*, p.149.
18 Jean Froissart (G. Brereton, trans. & ed.), *Chronicles*, (London: Penguin, 1978), p.410.

mainly kern) fighting for Lambert Simnel were slaughtered because they were unarmoured. There may be an element of scapegoating of the Irish for what was a bad plan from the start, but it may also be that kern, as light infantry, were misused and fielded badly by their commanders. Still, it is plain as a pikestaff that what Ireland lacked was middle-weight infantry who would be somewhere in between the kern and the galloglass in their equipment. Irish chiefs must have thought the solution lay with hiring Highland 'redshank' mercenaries, who were equipped in a manner which balanced protection and mobility, and who were available in large numbers. But to have foreign mercenaries as the bedrock of your army cannot have the long-term cohesiveness provided by soldiers fighting in defence of their own land.

Uniquely Vicious, or Simply Another Example of Military Disregard for Civilians?

Kern, then, were soldiers, guardsman and a security militia for the collection of taxes and for the enforcement of the chief's will, and there is no denying the frequent references to their bullying, intimidating behaviour. But would one of Strongbow's sergeants, or a Swiss mercenary, Welsh archer or English billman have been so very different? Jean Le Fèvre's account of the English or Welsh archers in Henry V's army (which he accompanied as a young man) could easily be a description of kern. Many of the archers, says Le

Lady Roesia de Verdun oversaw the building of Castleroche (or Castle Roche) in Co. Louth, for which she was congratulated by Henry III in 1236. Castleroche became an important frontier post for the English Pale. (drawing by F. Cannan-Braniff)

Fèvre, were 'without armour' and some had 'their feet naked.'[19] So probably the differences between a kern and an English or Welsh soldier were not that great, particularly after a few days in the field.

But writers biased towards England were good at moving the goal posts to safeguard the message that no true Englishman would commit atrocities. Thus, when Froissart tells us that some of the English army misbehaved in France and killed prisoners, he explains this away by claiming it was not actually Englishmen who misbehaved but naughty Cornishmen and Welshmen 'armed with long knives.'[20]

Even one of the most influential revisionist texts on medieval warfare falls back on the old stereotypes, such as the 'Scots, particularly the Highlanders, were barbaric fighters,'[21] and we often read in modern history books that the Irish did not take prisoners because they were 'barbarous.' An English sixteenth century compilation of poetry, the *Mirror for Magistrates*, expresses this deep-seated view that Irish armies pursued a form of total war in which they would kill and destroy rather than playing the game of war via ransom and negotiation:

> They know no law of armes, nor none will learne,
> They make not warre (as other doe) a play:
> The lord, the boy, the gallowglas, the kerne ....
> They saue no prisoners for ransome nor for pay: ....
> Theyr end of warre to see theyr enmy deade.[22]

The reality was different. Prisoners were taken, hostages being a prominent part of Irish political power-play. It is said that Tuathal Balbh (Tuathal 'tongue-tied'/'mute'), chieftain of the Ó Gallchobhair (or O'Gallagher) sept until his death in 1541, would only take prisoners in battle, and not kill, after he had heard a sermon by a friar.[23] Medieval Irish warfare was very stop-start and rarely an all-out fight to the finish. Indeed, one finds a recurring willingness among Gaelic Irish commanders to negotiate and build bridges – Ruaidrí Ua Conchobair, last High King of Ireland, appears to have been a skilful negotiator, compromise being 'typical of the High Kings.'[24]

The legality of war also mattered to Irish rulers. Art Mór Mac Murchadha, a charismatic commander, told Richard II that England's attempt to deprive

---

19   Quoted in M. Strickland, 'Chivalry at Agincourt,' in A. Curry (ed.), *Agincourt 1415: Henry V, Sir Thomas Erpingham and the Triumph of the English Archers* (Stroud: Tempus, 2000), p.115.
20   Froissart, *Chronicles*, p.93.
21   J. F. Verbruggen (S. Willard & R.W. Southern trans.), *The Art of Warfare in Western Europe During the Middle Ages* (Woodbridge: Boydell, 1998, revd edn), p.121.
22   J. Haslewood (ed.), *Mirror for Magistrates* (London, 1815), volume 2, p.30.
23   Gillespie, 'Gaelic Families of Donegal,' in Nolan, Ronayne & Dunlevy, *Donegal*, p.810.
24   Hayes-McCoy, *Irish Battles*, p.24.

him 'by conquest' of his status as 'rightful King of Ireland' was 'unlawful.'[25] Obviously, the fact that some Irish aristocrats were adept at diplomacy does not mean that the ordinary kern was much of a diplomat. The problem is rather that modern historians imply kern were vile pillagers as if this was the only way of war known to kern, and as if such behaviour was uniquely Gaelic, and not simply the appalling reality of all war.

Historians like a good story and it is customary to roll out the story of how horrified the French were by the behaviour of the Irishmen in Henry VIII's army in 1544. Stanihurst recounts that an Irishman in Henry's army called 'Nichol Welsh' swam a river to accept a challenge from a French soldier 'to bicker with him.' Welsh killed the Frenchman and then (less plausibly) returned to his own lines with the Frenchman's head 'in hys mouth.'[26] Doubtless some of these stories of Irish brutality are true or at least partly true. Yet it is surprising that so many modern historians accept without question accounts of Gaelic barbarism. These modern historians forget that military theorists such as Vegetius, a Roman whose advice for generals was held in high regard in the Middle Ages, would probably have thought that Henry VIII's kern did a good job of destroying France's economic strength by plundering and burning just about everything that would burn. Vegetius' cold advice was that to 'distress the enemy more by famine than the sword is a mark of consummate skill,' which puts a different light on the burning and theft of livestock typifying the kerns' military methods.[27]

Stanihurst was rather impressed by the scale of the destruction orchestrated by Henry VIII's Irish fighters who, says Stanihurst, were so useful at Henry's siege of Boulogne because they were not content to just 'burne and spoyle' the immediate area, but would 'rauage twentie or thirtie miles into the main lande.'[28] It goes without saying that such tactics are morally outrageous, but, rather than wanton vandalism, it is probably the case that this despoiling was a considered strategic choice. The harrying and despoiling tactics of kern are little different to the *chevauchée* tactics used by English and Welsh soldiers in the Hundred Years' War (or the French habit of wrecking English coastal towns). Given the effort that went into such operations (and the risks involved), one can only conclude that the spiteful savagery of laying waste to enemy territory by burning homes and stealing livestock as practised by medieval Irish, English, French and Scottish armies was a calculated tactic and not a loss of self-control or spontaneous savagery – or not always anyway.

The attitude of medieval Irish soldiers to civilians seems essentially the same as that which James O'Neill identified for the period of the Nine Years' War in Ireland: a callous disregard for civilians, and a belief that

---

25   Quoted in McGettigan, *Richard II*, pp.169–170.
26   Stanihurst, *Irish Chronicle*, p.303.
27   Flavius Vegetius Renatus (J. Clarke, trans.) *De Re Militari* (Milton Keynes: Leonaur, 2012), p.105.
28   Stanihurst, *Irish Chronicle*, p.302.

THE GAELIC WORLD AT WAR: SOLDIERS & SOLDIERING IN IRELAND 1366-1547

the civilians' needs are subordinate those of the military.[29] Perhaps some Irishmen were happy to play the part of the terrifying 'savage'; it would certainly be a good way to intimidate your opposition into submission. Born in London in 1477/1478, Thomas More imagined a society in his *Utopia* where fighting is largely outsourced to the 'Venalians' who, More says, are 'extremely primitive and savage,' 'very tough,' 'never do any farming,' and always looking for a fight.[30] Paul Turner proposed that More may actually have been thinking of the Swiss, and this may well be right.[31] But there are also echoes of Ireland here – especially when More tells us that the Utopians employ the wild Venalians because they are good fighters and because the enemy will do everyone a favour by killing the 'filthy scum' off.[32] This is eerily prescient of what Henry VIII ordered in 1545 when he decreed that 2,000 of the most 'savage' Irishmen should be recruited to fight against Scotland, since their absence 'should rather do good than hurt.'[33]

Crossbowman in the service of the Earl of Desmond, late 1400s. Historians sometimes give the impression that kern, galloglass, horsemen and redshank Scots were the only types of soldier in medieval Ireland. In fact, other troop types were present, including the crossbowmen known to have been in the Earl of Desmond's forces at the end of the fifteenth century. (Artwork by F. Cannan-Braniff)

---

29   J. O'Neill, *The Nine Years' War, 1593–1603: O'Neill, Mountjoy and the Military Revolution* (Dublin: Four Courts Press, 2017).
30   Thomas More (P. Turner, trans. and ed.), *Utopia* (London: Penguin, 2003), p.93.
31   More, *Utopia*, p.131, n. 33.
32   More, *Utopia*, p.94.
33   Quoted in S. G. Ellis, 'The Tudors and the Origins of the Modern Irish State: A Standing Army,' in Bartlett & Jeffery, *Military History of Ireland*, p.131.

Maybe the Fitzgerald Earls of Kildare thought More's *Utopia* might have some useful ideas for governance of their own domains – perhaps for ensuring violent families like the Keatings stayed loyal, or for governing vassals who did not wish to be ruled like the O'More (Ó Mórdha) lords of Laois – because within a decade of publication in 1516 they had acquired a copy for their library at their primary residence, Maynooth Castle.[34]

Neo-Classical Irish Soldiers?

Vegetius, as already noted, would probably have endorsed the scorched earth tactics of the kern, and there is, indeed, something distinctly Vegetian about the tripartite composition – horse, galloglass, kern – of late medieval Irish armies. Although by no means a perfect fit, when thinking about late medieval Irish armies one is reminded of Vegetius' description of a Roman legion. This bold claim needs to be understood in the light of the fact that, across Europe, medieval generals were very influenced by Vegetius' *De Re Militari* (*On Military Matters*), which was probably written in the late fourth century CE.

De Re Militari is easy to use, and whether you command 10 or 10,000 soldiers you will find something of interest to spark a discussion. The fact that *De Re Militari* is straightforward and has no complicated concepts may explain why it was so popular among medieval men of action. Copies of *De Re Militari* were available in the time of Charlemagne, Richard I of England took a copy on campaign, Caxton printed it in 1489, and Machiavelli knew about Vegetius' work. *De Re Militari* had earlier been available in manuscript form across much of Europe, sometimes in abridged versions, sometimes with different titles, and sometimes revised or reworked to highlight particular themes.[35]

So, one wonders, why not the marshals and constables of Gaelic armies, or their more literate staff? It is certainly possible to imagine Gaelic commanders reading Vegetius – or more likely hearing it read to them – and working out how they could make a kind of Irish Roman legion, the galloglass being the heavy foot, the kern the light foot, and the local aristocrats on horseback supplying the cavalry. Vegetius tells us (he seems to be harking back to the republic or early imperial Roman period) that a 'complete Roman legion' contains several types of soldier which we can clarify as:

---

34 D. Ó Catháin, 'Some Reflexes of Latin Learning and of the Renaissance in Ireland c. 1450-c. 1600,' in J. Harris & K. Sidwell (eds.), *Making Ireland Roman: Irish Neo-Latin Writers and the Republic of Letters* (Togher: Cork University Press, 2009), pp.23 & 25.

35 See Vegetius, *De Re Militari*, introduction.

A) 'heavy-armed foot' (including first-line *principes,* second-line *hastati,* and third-line *triarii,* as well as *antesignani* who, Vegetius says, are responsible for 'the proper exercises and discipline')
B) 'light-armed foot' (comprising *ferentarii* [skirmishers], archers, slingers')
C) artillery (*balistarii*)
D) 'legionary cavalry'[36]

Galloglass as Gaelic *Triarii?* Vegetian Theory in Ireland

Vegetius recommends that 'the *triarii*, completely armed' should be drawn up at the rear of your army, and have a particularly important role to play.[37] The English antiquary and herald William Camden included the damning statement in *Britannia* (first published in Latin in 1586) that the Ireland of his day was 'altogether voide of any polite and exquisite literature.'[38] The reason it is impossible to accept this assertion is that Camden's own book uses that same Latin word to describe the battlefield role of galloglass: '… *triariis, quos galoglassios appellant, qui securibus utuntur acutissimis.*'[39] Triarii often meant the troops stationed in the third line, but it could also denote reserves more generally, and so the first English-language edition of *Britannia* (published 1610) translates this passage as: '*souldiers set in the rere gard, whom they terme* Galloglasses…'[40] Another way of translating the same is: '… the reserves, which they call galloglass, and who fight with the sharpest axes.'[41]

Whatever your preferred translation, *Britannia* has inadvertently prompted us into making a comparison between the Irish Gaeltacht and that supposed pinnacle of martial practice, the Roman army. We know Vegetius was written and thought about in medieval England and Scotland through manuscript copies in Latin and reworkings and then translations, the earliest known English translation of *De Re Militari* being completed 1408, and an 'ynglis' translation of parts of '*Vegius de rei militari*' was made by a Scottish herald named Adam Loutfut in 1494.[42] But the medieval Irish

---

36   Vegetius, *De Re Militari*, pp.40, 44.
37   Vegetius, *De Re Militari*, pp. 51-53.
38   William Camden, *Britannia*, a hypertext edition of the 1607 and 1610 translation by Philemon Holland with notes by D.F. Sutton and available online at The Philological Museum, within section on 'The Maners of the Irishry.'
39   Camden, *Britannia*, at Philological Museum.
40   Camden, *Britannia*, at Philological Museum.
41   Edmund Gibson's 1772 translation of *Britannia* rendered the passage as: 'Their armies consist of horsemen, and of veteran [*triariis*] soldiers reserved for the rear (whom they call galloglasses, and who fight with sharp hatchets…'. William Camden (E. Gibson, trans. and ed.), *Britannia* (London, 1772), volume 2, p.380.
42   C. Allmand, *The De Re Militari of Vegetius: The Reception, Transmission and Legacy*

were more learned and less cut off than many imagine, and they knew of Vegetius too. 'Vegesius' appears in a list made in 1526 of the Earl of Kildare's books (and/or manuscripts) at Maynooth Castle.[43] Vegetius is not listed in what appears to be an earlier catalogue of Kildare's books, so perhaps this was a recent acquisition.[44] Until the castle was seized by the English in 1535, Maynooth's library also had works by classical authors (some with obvious military interest) including Caesar, Ovid, Cicero and Vergil.[45]

One important medieval reworking of Vegetius was made by the Venetian-born writer Christine de Pisan and the Earls of Kildare also owned a copy of this work. Pisan, who was born in 1364, blended Vegetian theory on military organisation with a plea for strong leadership, national unity and the need for imperturbable 'constables' to command your forces. Kildare's staff catalogued Pisan's book as 'The Feetis of Armes of Chyvalry, made by Christ. de Pyze.'[46] From this we surmise Kildare owned an English translation, most likely that printed in 1489/90 by William Caxton as *The Book of Fayttes of Armes and of Chyvalrye*. If this is the edition that Kildare owned, it means he had obtained a copy while the book was still current, contemporary reading.

Two limestone cannonballs found in Galway city; perhaps fourteenth to seventeenth century. (From J. Higgins, Galway's Heritage in Stone)

---

  of a Roman Text in the Middle Ages (Cambridge: Cambridge University Press, 2013), pp.185 & 235.
43 Ó Catháin, 'Some Reflexes,' in Harris & Sidwell, *Making Ireland Roman*, pp.22–23.
44 Ó Catháin, 'Some Reflexes,' in Harris & Sidwell, *Making Ireland Roman*, pp.22–23.
45 Ó Catháin, 'Some Reflexes,' in Harris & Sidwell, *Making Ireland Roman*, pp.22–24.
46 H. F. Hore, 'Life in Old Ireland' in *Ulster Journal of Archaeology*, first series, volume 7 (1859), p.277.

In other words, Vegetian theory was lodged in the library of one of Ireland's most powerful families, the Fitzgeralds of Kildare. Perhaps few people ever read the Irish, English, French and Latin-language works in the Kildare library. Perhaps it was all there just to create a look of cultivation. But Maynooth was not the only library in Ireland.[47] Furthermore, medieval Irish scholars working abroad were aware of Vegetius. The Irish scholar Sedulius Scotus, who settled in Liège in the mid-ninth century, made a manuscript including 25 excerpts from *De Re Militari*,[48] and Thomas of Ireland ('Thomas Hibernicus'), an Irish-born cleric at the Sorbonne, cites Vegetius in his early fourteenth century work, *Manipulus Florum*.[49]

Thomas and Sedulius may have been more interested in the moral and religious questions raised by Vegetius' work, but Trinity College Dublin has a manuscript, probably made in the second half of the fifteenth century, very likely in England and possibly in East Anglia, of parts of Vegetius where the emphasis is more on developing soldierly excellence.[50] Given its apparent origin it may be that the Trinity manuscript, in which Vegetius features as part of a compilation of classical literature, originally had an English rather than Irish owner. On the other hand, it has evidently been in Ireland a long time: Samuel Foley, a Church of Ireland bishop and Fellow of Trinity College Dublin born in 1655, has made notes on the manuscript.[51] An earlier hand has made notes on the manuscript too, including *Nota bene*, and *de werra Scottorum* ('on the Scottish war') next to Vegetius' statement that 'armies are more often destroyed by starvation than by battle,'[52] surely a warning about logistical difficulties English armies would face campaigning in Scotland.

Perhaps, then, instead of imagining galloglass as axe-wielding berserkers, we should think of them as acting like heavily-equipped Roman legionary *triarii*: steady heavy infantry who can be relied upon to keep formation and wait their turn during the confusion of battle, and perform such disciplined actions as delivering the decisive assault against the enemy, or, should

---

47 The library of the Franciscan Order at Youghal had French and German texts and was catalogued between 1491 and 1523. Callan's Augustinian friary (Co. Kilkenny) is said to have had a good library, and the Franciscan Third Order at Slane (Co. Meath) may also have had a library. Ó Catháin, 'Some Reflexes,' in Harris & Sidwell, *Making Ireland Roman*, pp.17, 24, 200 n. 58, 201 n. 76. It would be very surprising if the Fitzgeralds of Desmond and the Butlers of Ormond did not have their own libraries; part of the payment for the ransom for Edmund MacRichard Butler (taken prisoner by Desmond forces at the Battle of Piltown) consisted of two Irish manuscripts: Morgan, 'Pilltown,' *OCIH*.
48 Allmand, *The De Re Militari*, p.213.
49 Allmand, *The De Re Militari*, p.217; 'Thomas of Ireland (Thomas Hibernicus),' *DIB* (entry by A. Breen).
50 IE TCD MS 632, ff.128–129v; Allmand, *The De Re Militari*, pp.221–222.
51 A. Chahoud & E. Stagni, 'A Pseudo-Classical Dialogue in TCD MS 632,' *Hermathena*, no. 194 (summer 2013), pp.153–154; TCD website: library catalogue entry for MS 632; 'Foley, Samuel,' *DIB* (entry by L. Lunney).
52 Allmand, *The De Re Militari*, p.222.

things go wrong, to conduct an orderly fighting rearguard. Likewise, kern do not have to be seen as harrying and skirmishing because they were too stupid to put on armour or understand battlefield tactics – but because this, as neo-classical *ferentarii*, was their intended military role. Vegetius tells us that the 'ancients' selected their light foot from the 'most active' and disciplined men; to have been efficient raiders kern must assuredly have had those qualities.

Even for a warrior with no interest in book-learning, it would have been easy enough to pick up bits of military theory from English and Welsh soldiers – even if learned the hard way by fighting against them. English and Welsh soldiers also served as mercenaries in Irish armies, and the 1st Earl of Desmond (died 1356) recruited not just kern but Anglo-Irish outlaws as soldiers.[53] Post-reformation, there were still ample opportunities to discuss military and political developments with Englishmen via renegades and adventurers such as Thomas Stucley (a pirate who mixed with Irish lords including Shane O'Neill), Thomas Lee (ex-highwayman turned soldier who had his portrait painted as an officer of kern) and Father Nicholas Sander (who, educated at Winchester and Oxford, became an important figure in the Desmond rising against Elizabeth I).

It would, in short, be extremely surprising if the better commanders in a book-loving country like Ireland did not hone their craft by consulting works of military theory.[54] There is plenty of evidence for learning (or at least respect for learning) among the late medieval Irish nobility,[55] clergy,[56] and even galloglass clans.[57] We also know military texts existed in Ireland

---

53 J. Lydon, 'The Scottish Soldier Abroad: The Bruce Invasion and the Galloglass,' in S. Duffy (ed.), *Robert the Bruce's Irish Wars: The Invasions of Ireland 1306–1329* (Stroud: Tempus, 2002), p.102.

54 After all, who can forget that the first translator of *Don Quixote*, Thomas Shelton, was a Dublin Catholic who worked for the anti-English cause?

55 For instance, the Munster chief Fingin O'Mahoney (Ó Mathgamna) made his own translation into Irish of 'Travels of Sir John Mandeville' in the fifteenth century: I. M. Higgins, *Writing East: The 'Travels' of Sir John Mandeville* (Philadelphia: University of Pennsylvania Press, 1997), p.59; Simms, *Gaelic Ulster*, p.429. The 8th Earl of Desmond was said to understand Irish, English and Latin, and tried to start a university at Drogheda in the mid-1460s. The 3rd Earl of Desmond was a poet in Irish and possibly French: Ó Catháin, 'Some Reflexes,' in Harris & Sidwell, *Making Ireland Roman*, pp.20–21.

56 Medieval Ireland's best clergy could be highly educated and international, and exactly the sort of person who knew about Vegetius. The Archbishop of Tuam, Muiris Ó Ficheallaigh, who died in Galway in 1513, was educated at Oxford and in Italy, and had been Professor of Theology at Padua University, Ó Catháin, 'Some Reflexes,' in Harris & Sidwell, *Making Ireland Roman*, pp.19–20.

57 Máire, the wife of Ruaidhrí Mac Suibhne Fanad, owned a book of religious tracts and saints' lives, and with her husband founded Rathmullan Friary in the 1500s. They did this, it is said, to honour their son, also called Ruaidhrí, who had travelled abroad and spoke many languages: so galloglass were not necessarily uneducated thugs. See Gillespie, 'Gaelic Families' in Nolan, Ronayne & Dunlevy, *Donegal*, p.781; K. Simms, 'Images of the Galloglass in Poems to the MacSweeneys' in S.

in the late 1500s. Barnabe Rich, an English infantryman and writer who was largely based in Ireland 1573–1592, read military manuals, Spanish soldiers stationed in Ireland in the 1580s had Continental military books with them, and George Carew, an able but hard soldier from Devon who became governor of Munster, was presented with a book on fortification.[58] Printing had by then made it easier to share such ideas, Garret Barry, an Irishman who joined the Spanish army around 1601, was among the writers of military texts which appeared in the seventeenth century. But there is no evidence that the printing press *created* an interest in military theory in Ireland or anywhere else.

Drawn After the Quick: The Use & Misuse of Early Images of Irish Soldiers

Once one shakes off the prejudice that premodern Ireland and Scotland were void of literature and learning it becomes possible to see early depictions of Irish people for what they really are. Too many historians include early images of Irish people in their publications simply to give a 'bit of colour,' without providing careful analysis, as if the images speak for themselves or

The Rock of Cashel in Co. Tipperary, seat of the kings of Munster. (Artwork by F. Cannan-Braniff)

Duffy (ed.), *The World of the Galloglass: Kings, Warlords and Warriors in Ireland and Scotland, 1200–1600* (Dublin: Four Courts Press, 2007), p.106; P. Walsh, *Leabhar Chlainne Suibhne: An Account of the MacSweeney Families in Ireland* (Dublin: Dollard, 1920), p.xxviii.

58 'Rich, Barnaby (Barnabe)', *DIB* (entry by A. M. McCormack & T. Clavin); D. R. Lawrence, *The Complete Soldier: Military Books and Military Culture in Early Stuart England, 1603–1645* (Leiden: Brill, 2009), p.77.

can be accepted as gospel for the appearance of the Irish for the entirety of the medieval and early modern periods.[59]

The Ashmolean Museum has an anonymous hand-coloured woodcut which has the potential to be one of the most important early representations of Irish warriors if, as the text running along the top of the woodcut declares, it really was made from life. The woodcut's provenance is that it was transferred to the Ashmolean from the Bodleian Library in 1863. The Bodleian acquired the woodcut in 1834 from Francis Douce. Born in 1757, Douce was Keeper of the Manuscripts at the British Museum and a collector of early books and manuscripts. In his will, Douce (who died in 1834) left most of his collection to the Bodleian.

As for the woodcut's date, the artist's style, the style of Irish dress and the font used for the text 'DRAVN AFTER THE QVICKE' running across the top of the picture all suggest it was made in the sixteenth century. Historians have dated the woodcut to the reign of Henry VIII but, in short, there is nothing to permit such precision. Ashmolean staff believe it may be late sixteenth century, and that it could be based on three coloured drawings (one in the British Library, two in Ghent University Library) of Irish people by the artist Lucas de Heere (1534–1584).[60]

De Heere was a Flemish Protestant who worked in England for a decade from the mid to late 1560s (different historians give slightly different dates).[61] There are many differences in dress, age, gender and posture between the Ashmolean woodcut and de Heere's illustrations. But there are also important similarities. In one of the Ghent University de Heere images an Irishman wears his cloak over his head, something we see in the Ashmolean's woodcut. An anxious-looking bearded Irishman in the British Library's de Heere image perhaps resembles the third figure from left in the Ashmolean woodcut (also bearded but this time smiling). The young man with a jacket and sword in the same Ghent University image also seems similar to the man on the far left of the Ashmolean woodcut.

De Heere was probably a better artist than the anonymous printmaker who made the Ashmolean woodcut – but that does not mean de Heere is the original and Ashmolean is the copy. Perhaps it was the other way around.[62] The Ashmolean image is carefully depicted and appears accurate, with the exception of the inflated size of the swords. If the Ashmolean woodcut was

---

59 See Hiram Morgan on the uses and misuses of Derricke's *Image of Irelande*: 'Derrick, John,' *OCIH*. Again, the Tate portrait of Thomas Lee is not simply a man dressed as a kern, but is thought to be a reference to Livy – 'Lee, Thomas,' *DIB* (entry by J. Barry).
60 Ashmolean Museum object file.
61 Dates taken from J. T. Dunbar, *History of Highland Dress* (London: Batsford, 1978), pp.51–52; T. Willis, 'A Two Handed Gaelic Irish Sword of the Sixteenth Century,' *The Fifteenth Park Lane Arms Fair* (1998), p.21; and information on websites of Royal Collections and British Museum.
62 Willis asked the same question in 'A Two Handed Gaelic Irish Sword,' pp.21–22.

made from life, then it ranks as an extremely important piece of evidence – surely more so than Dürer's skilful reconstruction of Irish soldiers.

Or indeed de Heere's. After all, what Irish people did de Heere see? Text on one de Heere image says it shows 'Irlandois et Irlandoise' serving 'Roy Henry' – which must mean Henry VIII who had hired kern for use against France and Scotland. But that was in 1544–1545, more than a decade before de Heere moved to England. They could be Keating kern contracted by the government in the second half of the sixteenth century, but how would de Heere, based in England, have seen them? There had been kern in London in 1550,[63] and Shane O'Neill's posse were in London in 1562 – but, again, this was probably before de Heere was in England. One begins to suspect de Heere did not draw his picture 'after the quick,' and, as probably with the 1521 Dürer image, it is a renaissance artist's impression of Irish people based on oral testimony and/or written and pictorial sources. De Heere's illustrations were for a book about Britain and Ireland, possibly as a guide for Flemish Protestant refugees.[64] We do not know the Ashmolean woodcut's intended audience, and though it may date from Henry VIII's reign, it remains just as likely that it dates from the reign of Edward, Mary or Elizabeth.

Perhaps the Ashmolean woodcut is also a 'simulation' of Irish dress by an artist who had never actually seen an Irishman. The woodcut's Irishmen look ragged because the artist has not successfully depicted the texture, thickness and shaggy edging of their traditional Gaelic cloaks. That kind of hesitancy in an artwork can be a sign of fakery. One's thoughts return to Dürer's representation of Irishmen, which, as Hiram Morgan has argued, seems unlikely to have been made from life.[65] The unnamed female artist mentioned at the start of this book wondered which was the galloglass, and while she surely opted for the wrong figure, none of the figures seem likely to be primary source material for the appearance of galloglass. Dürer achieved the appearance of authenticity in his image of Irishmen because he was a great artist, not because he had seen Irishmen.

Historians become bewitched by the images showing what they think are quintessential Irish costume and manners, without understanding that they might well be looking at early ethnographic studies intended for gawping renaissance intellectuals abroad which, more often than not, were probably assemblages of travellers' gossip and tittle-tattle. The art that was based on eyewitness testimony (such as the illustration of Art Mór Mac Murchadha on horseback in Creton's account) or was made by Irish craftspeople for Irish audiences – be it aristocratic commissions like the 'Book of the de Burgos' or amateur scribblings on a basement wall – shows a more diverse, and sometimes completely different styles of dress, armament and haircut.

---

63   *OED*, 'Kern,' under the year 1550.
64   J. T. Dunbar, *History of Highland Dress* (London: Batsford, 1978), pp.51–52.
65   H. Morgan, 'Sunday 6 June 1518 – the Day the Renaissance Came to Ireland,' *History Ireland* (May/June 2012).

CEITHEARNACH: IRELAND'S 'ORDINARY SOLDIER' REIMAGINED

The basement wall in question is at Enniscorthy Castle, Wexford, where an incised figure of a man survives.[66] The figure is unclear; possibly he holds a sword, possibly he wears a smart suit of sixteenth century clothes; but either way he in no way conforms to stereotypes of Irish dress.

Crude and frustratingly unclear, the Enniscorthy figure seems to belong to the same world of clothing depicted in other little-known Irish art such as a late fifteenth century stone window spandrel from Galway city showing a piper dressed in a thick pleated doublet, and possibly hose.[67] Or the stone fragment, probably late fifteenth/early sixteenth century, and again from Galway city, of a man apparently wearing a fashionable codpiece and short breeches.[68] Both of the Galway figures wear fitted clothes and have short hair – not at all the long-haired, bare-legged tribesmen in billowing tunics, cloaks and robes foreign audiences wanted to see. Or consider the archers in their neat jackets in the fresco at Knockmoy Abbey, Galway; before the paint faded, it was recorded that the archers had greenish jackets, yellow hose and black shoes.[69] Perhaps this was a family livery. We do not have to believe Gaelic aristocrats were too disordered or impoverished to come up with a colour scheme for their retainers, or that every Irish soldier always wore a saffron shirt.

Enniscorthy Castle, Wexford, shown on a hand-coloured print of 1792. (Author's Collection)

---

66   R. Sherlock, 'Report on 'The Halberdier Wall Painting'' (archaeological survey for Enniscorthy Castle, available on the Castle's website).
67   J. Higgins, *Galway's Heritage in Stone*, Galway City Museum catalogue no. 1 (Galway: Galway City Museum, 2006), cat. no. 10.
68   Higgins, *Galway's Heritage*, cat. no. 5.
69   M. Dunlevy, *Dress in Ireland: A History* (Wilton: Doughcloyne, 1999), caption to fig. 18.

THE GAELIC WORLD AT WAR: SOLDIERS & SOLDIERING IN IRELAND 1366-1547

Unarmoured?

Of course, saffron shirts and short jackets were worn – after all, the English tried to ban Irish dress because they knew it to be a symbol of cultural pride. But Irish dress and military equipment was clearly always diverse, evolving and regional. Because there is not much evidence of body defence in images such as the Ashmolean woodcut, historians rush to the judgement that kern, as a rule, did not wear armour or even helmets. The problem with this view is that it seems to presuppose kern were some kind of modern, uniformed force all using the same equipment, all across Ireland, all through the Middle Ages.[70] Even a brief glance at the sources shows this view to be too dogmatic and definitive.

Clearly armour was not worn by all kern, or even most kern, but it was definitely worn sometimes. The sixteenth century Cowdray House mural of the siege of Boulogne in 1544 is lost, but an eighteenth century engraving of the mural appears to show kern wearing helmets. Marcus Gheeraerts' portrait of Thomas Lee,[71] who died in 1601 after extensive service in Ireland, shows Lee dressed as a kern with a helmet and shield for protection (and his thick waistcoat might also give some defence). True, the Ashmolean woodcut shows five out of the six Irishmen without any armour – but, crucially, we do not know if they are kern in battle-dress, off-duty kern, horsemen, galloglass or something else.[72] A focussed, detailed description of kern is, however, provided by the scholar, diplomat and medicinal potion-maker Richard Stanihurst, who was born in Dublin in 1547. Stanihurst defines 'kerns' as 'light-armed swordsmen' who 'whirl spears, which are fitted with thongs' (i.e. javelins), throw stones and hack and slash rather than thrust with their swords.[73] According to Stanihurst kern were protected by 'short shields or iron gauntlets,' and when 'going into battle' they 'wear no *heavy* armour' [my italics].[74]

The chronicles of Froissart include the observation that the Irish (most of whom were probably kern) who clashed with Richard II's army at the end of the fourteenth century wore 'very simple' armour.[75] We are not told if this relates to all Irish soldiers, or just one type of soldier, but 'very simple' armour is not the same as no armour. Simple armour makes one think of leather or quilted garments, jacks, short mail shirts, coifs (and later, mantles), gauntlets or gloves, leather-covered round shields, light helmets,

---

70 More bizarre is the claim made by modern writers that only the gentry in a Highland army would have worn armour. This is not what the evidence shows.
71 In the collection of Tate Britain.
72 The only armour in the woodcut is a metal gauntlet worn by a man performing a blocking move. He also wears something substantial on his head, but this is probably a woollen cap.
73 Stanihurst, *Great Deeds*, p.125.
74 Stanihurst, *Great Deeds*, p.125.
75 Froissart, *Chronicles*, pp.410, 412.

metal 'splints' on the arms. 'Unarmoured' is an oversimplification; 'lightly armoured,' 'lightly protected' or even 'poorly armoured' is perhaps nearer the mark.

The War of the Worlds Fallacy

Froissart and Stanihurst's descriptions show we are not obliged to think of kern as pitifully equipped tribesmen. We are free to consider kern as warriors who understand that heavy armour will reduce their effectiveness as light infantry. Descriptions of Irish armour (or lack of) must be analysed with care since, once again, there is a degree of anti-Irish bias. Gerald of Wales implies it is the absence of armour which shows the Irish to be backward, but John Derricke says in *The Image of Irelande* that it is the wearing of armour which shows the Irish to be backward – this time because they wear it too often as normal clothing, wearing 'sculles' (the term for a simple bowl-shaped helmet) 'In steade of civill Cappes.'[76] In the background to all of this is the fallacy that medieval England and medieval Ireland were two technologically different worlds, and that kern were barefoot Iron Age leftovers who stood no chance against the (literal) mailed fist of England.

The English or Anglo-Norman assault on Ireland in the 1100s is to this day presented by historians as if it were a kind of *War of the Worlds*-style alien invasion, between 'rough and primitive'[77] Irish foot soldiers and 'infinitely better armed'[78] knights whose equipment was 'light years ahead of the Irish.'[79]

Flanagan has demonstrated that there are serious problems with this mental picture of the English invasion of Ireland.[80] The truth about the English is that they were from another country, not another world. Some of the claims about Irish warriors going, 'naked and unarmed into battle' are clearly disingenuous exaggerations.[81] There is no doubt that armour was owned by the Irish before the English invasion. Chroniclers' claims, to this day repeated by modern historians, that it was Scandinavians who introduced the battle-axe to Ireland, and that it was the 'Normans' (i.e. English and Welsh) who introduced the Irish to metal armour, are impossible to take seriously.

---

76 John Derricke (F. J. Sypher, ed.), *The Image of Irelande: With a Discouerie of Woodkarne* (Delmar: Scholars' Facsimiles & Reprints, 1998. Original edition, London: 1581), p.49.
77 Verbruggen, *Art of Warfare*, p.57.
78 Verbruggen, *Art of Warfare*, p.48.
79 T. Asbridge, *The Greatest Knight* (London: Simon & Schuster, 2015), p.292.
80 Flanagan, 'Irish and Anglo-Norman Warfare,' in Bartlett & Jeffery, *Military History of Ireland*, pp.52–75.
81 Gerald of Wales (J. J. O'Meara, trans.), *The History and Topography of Ireland* (London: Penguin, 1982), p.101.

THE GAELIC WORLD AT WAR: SOLDIERS & SOLDIERING IN IRELAND 1366-1547

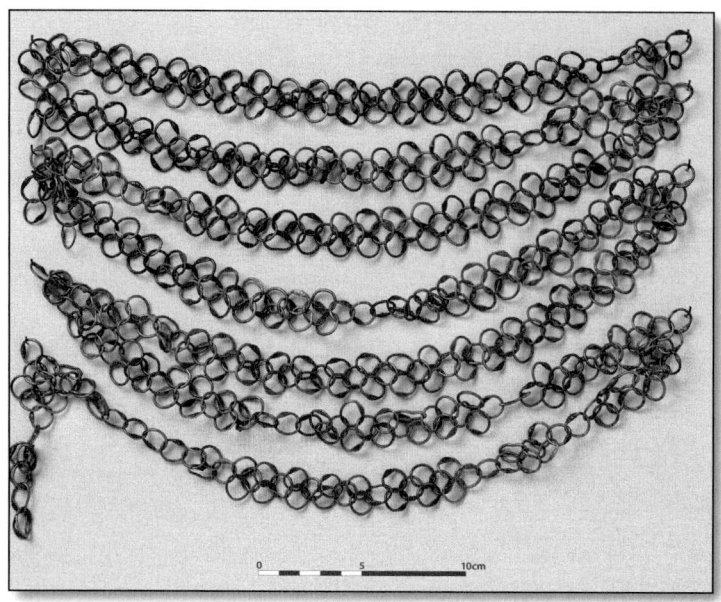

Not much armour with an Irish provenance survives, and this band of riveted mail has a dual interest for the medievalist. On the one hand, it is a rare piece of surviving mail in Ireland. On the other, it is evidence for the use of armour as sacred charms in Ireland. This mail band and a crozier are recorded as having been presented to the antiquary and artist George Petrie (d. 1866) by a Mr Woods of Sligo. One account claims this mail band and the crozier were considered relics of St Mura, patron saint of the Ó Néill dynasty. There is, however, a possibility that the mail band and crozier come from the church of St Lommán of Portloman, Lough Owel in Co. Westmeath, where a crozier and chain of Lommán's are recorded; this chain was wrapped around women to heal and protect them during childbirth. The mail band itself, described as being 'bronze' or 'brass,' measures 2.4 metres in length. An uneven number of rings have been used, suggesting pieces are missing and giving the impression that this might be the remnant of a larger piece – perhaps even a garment. We know that the Mac Suibhne sept of Boghaineach (Banagh) had the responsibility of providing a man to carry the charmstone and 'lúirigh' (*luireach* is the usual Gaelic term for a mail shirt) of their patron saint, Colum Cille. (© National Museum of Ireland)

Some descriptions of Irish nakedness were meant literally, such as when Sir Anthony St Leger, appointed Lord Deputy of Ireland in 1540, reported to the King that kern were often 'bare nakyd' when they had a 'bycker,' having stripped to the waist ('bicker', incidentally, is an excellent description of the kern's style, since the word originally meant skirmish, attack with repeated blows or wrangle).[82] At other times naked or unarmed meant soldiers were badly equipped or were effectively 'naked' in comparison with their heavily-equipped opponents. And so, Christian crusaders are described in French verse of *c.* 1195 as 'very well armed' while Muslim soldiers are supposedly 'unarmed.'[83]

---

82 Quoted in E.D. Borrowes, 'Tennekille Castle, Portarlington, and Glimpses of the MacDonnells' in *Ulster Journal of Archaeology*, 1st series, volume 2 (1854), p.41. For 'bicker' see *OED*. Fighting shirtless is reminiscent of the Highland combatants at 1544's 'Battle of the Shirts'.

83 Quoted in Verbruggen, *Art of Warfare*, p.61.

CEITHEARNACH: IRELAND'S 'ORDINARY SOLDIER' REIMAGINED

Perhaps early Irish storytellers liked the notion of unprotected Irish soldiers as a way to highlight the heroic hardiness of the Irish over the Scandinavians, the implications being that the Irish were too brave to hide behind armour, or too skilful to need armour, or possibly that they did not need body amour because they wear the spiritual armour of God's blessing.[84] As is so often the case in the history of war, technological differences are a wholly unconvincing explanation for the English conquest of Ireland.[85] Irish soldiers fought both and for and against the English knights who entered Ireland in the 1100s; the situation was not a clear war between nationalities.[86]

The traditional view of the Anglo-Norman 'conquest' moreover assumes soldiers used the same equipment for all types of warfare. This is unlikely. Soldiers, whether Irish, English or Welsh, would have worn their heaviest armour for pitched battles, changing into lighter equipment for raids. Given that raiding and skirmishing were more common events in medieval Ireland than pitched battles, one begins to wonder whether, in reality, Irish, English and Welsh soldiers were often wearing fairly similar equipment. Supporting this hypothesis is what happened at the Battle of Dysert O'Dea in 1318. The battle was fought in Co. Clare between the Anglo-Irish marcher lord, Richard de Clare, and the Gaelic King of Thomond, Muirchertach Ó Briain (O'Brien). But when Irish reinforcements arrived, Ó Briain's army were at first unable to tell which side they were on.[87]

It is also important to remember that most kern would not have worn any kind of uniform – 'most' because it is conceivable that those serving the wealthiest lords like the Butlers of Ormond or the Desmond and Kildare Fitzgeralds may have worn liveries or colours or at least badges. However, when choosing battlefield equipment, kern would have been free to use whatever equipment they wanted within the parameters of what they, or their lord, could buy, barter, salvage, make or steal.

A Burke (Bourke, de Burgh, de Búrca) nobleman and dog in the sixteenth century 'Book of the de Burgos.' His open-faced helmet with aventail and mail shirt are characteristically Gaelic, and a combination that remained popular with Irish and Highland Scottish soldiers throughout the late Middle Ages and Renaissance. The red feature around the brim of his barbute helmet may be a twisted cloth band. (The Board of Trinity College Dublin)

---

84 Flanagan, 'Irish and Anglo-Norman Warfare,' in Bartlett & Jeffery, *Military History of Ireland*, p.54. Even seemingly simple words in medieval accounts of warfare can be embedded with agendas: as C. Tyerman explored in *How to Plan a Crusade: Reason and Religious War in the High Middle Ages* (London: Penguin, 2016), pp.170–177, how words like 'the poor' and 'poverty' in accounts of crusader armies may be at times be relative and even metaphorical.

85 See Flanagan, 'Irish and Anglo-Norman Warfare,' in Bartlett & Jeffery, *Military History of Ireland*.

86 Flanagan, 'Irish and Anglo-Norman Warfare,' p.67.

87 Hayes-McCoy, *Irish Battles*, p.45.

Poverty or lack of foreign imports is used by historians to explain the lightness of Irish battle-dress. Ireland was indeed a relatively poor nation and supply was not always easy; fourteenth century English legislation forbade the supply of horses and military equipment to the Gaelic Irish.[88] But it is incorrect to imagine Irish lords were too poor to acquire armour. When St Leger met Manus Ó Domhnaill, ruler of Tír Chonaill, in 1541, Manus did not look like a barbarian chieftain but rather a prince in a crimson velvet jacket, fine cloak and bonnet.[89] Ireland's richest individual, the 9th Earl of Kildare, was among the 10 wealthiest Tudor nobles, his annual income exceeding £2,000 (Irish).[90] The Earls of Ormond were also very rich, both from land and from receiving a lucrative tax on wine imported into Ireland, and possibly also, after 1375, from silver and lead mines.[91] In 1503, the Earl of Desmond was reported to have a mine, in his case for gold.[92] Less powerful chiefs than Kildare, Ormond and Desmond still often had impressive wealth, probably mainly from agriculture. Sir Brian Ó Néill, Lord of Lower Clandeboye from 1556, reputedly had 30,000 cattle, as well as sheep and pigs.[93] That is comparable to the number of livestock said to have been owned by Hugh Despenser, one of England's most powerful men during the reign of Edward II.[94] It would not have been a problem for an Irish landowner with that kind of wealth to buy, whether with coin or animals, a few jacks or shoes for his kern.[95]

A letter of 1537 to Thomas Cromwell from a rather unscrupulous official in Ireland named Robert Cowley mentions galloglass captains having

---

88 'Warfare,' *OCIH* (entry by K. Simms).
89 B. Lacey's introduction to Manus O'Donnell (B. Lacey, ed.), *The Life of Colum Cille* (Dublin: Four Courts Press, 1994), p.10.
90 S. G. Ellis, 'The Tudor Borderlands, 1485–1603' in J. Morrill (ed.), *The Oxford Illustrated History of Tudor & Stuart Britain* (Oxford: Oxford University Press, 1996), p.67; 'FitzGerald, Gerald (Gearóid Óg, Garrett McAlison),' *DIB* (entry by M.A. Lyons).
91 'Butler, Thomas,' *DIB* (entry by D. Edwards); M. B. Deevy, *Medieval Ring Brooches in Ireland* (Bray: Wordwell), p.41.
92 Deevy, *Medieval Ring Brooches*, p.41.
93 H. F. Hore, 'Life in Old Ireland', p.274.
94 John Stow, *A Survey of London Written in the Year 1598*, ed. H. Morley (Stroud: Sutton, 1999), p.113.
95 It is forgotten how aspects of the medieval manorial way of life persisted into relatively late times in Ireland. Maria Edgeworth's novel of aristocratic Irish life in the days of George III, *Castle Rackrent* (published in 1800) shows how Irish landowners were able to live grandly without a great need for hard currency because labour was cheap and because they got much of what they needed for free. Castle Rackrent's rascally old steward waxes about how the lady of the manor gets all her linen spun, woven and bleached from the locals for nothing, and her food for 'next to nothing,' as the tenants never think of coming near the castle without giving 'a present of something or other – nothing too much or too little for my lady – eggs – honey – butter – meal – fish – game, growse, and herrings, fresh or salt,' among other foods, and as for the tenants' pigs and chickens, 'we had them.' D. Watson (ed.), *Castle Rackrent* (Oxford: OUP, 2008), pp.13–14.

stockpiles of mail shirts.[96] Why would a kern captain be any different? Irish castles must have had armouries, but these have not been studied. Even if a captain of kern had no money or access to merchants who would trade with him, he had plenty of able skirmishers to steal equipment for him. Besides, as any resourceful re-enactor will testify, one does not need money to make body armour; all that is needed are some scraps, a little ingenuity and time. Of course there was poverty and shortage of supplies in Ireland, but there was also intelligent tactical choice, and a bit of turning a material disadvantage into a military strength. If you are the kind of person who would prefer to wear trousers and full plate armour, then you are probably not the kind of person a captain of kern was looking to recruit.

---

96 *State Papers, Vol. II: King Henry the Eighth, Part 3* (1834), p.448.

2

Gallóglach: Perspectives on the Axeman

> Gallowglasses.... Being human for them is to be a hater of humanity!
>
> Stanihurst, *Great Deeds in Ireland*

Faces stare from a book. The book, known as the 'Book of the de Burgos,' is in the library of Trinity College Dublin and was made for Seaan, 17th Lord of the Mac Uilliam Íochtair Burkes, who died in 1580.[1] Written in Gaelic and Latin, the book is illustrated with images of Burke noblemen and Christ's Passion, which, although a world away from the technical finish of Dürer, are full of character and interest for the historian.

One of the illustrations shows Christ, mocked and bloodied, carrying the cross through the streets of Jerusalem.[2] Along with several other figures, four Roman soldiers surround Christ. The polearm of a fifth juts above the crowd. But the soldiers do not look Roman, for they are modelled on Irish soldiers at the close of the Middle Ages. Wearing tall, pointed helmets of late medieval vintage, and protected by mail over their shoulders, these 'Roman' soldiers carry polearms quite unlike the 'pilum' of old. Some hold thick-shafted spears, while one figure in the left foreground grips a long-handled battle-axe. Their mail armour has gold-coloured bands representing decorative edging of brass or bronze rings.

One soldier at the top right hand of the picture looks to be a big military man, standing straight and upright, his face stern and devoid of sympathy. The soldier in the left foreground, however, seems to watch the scene with more concern. Perhaps there is even a trace of misgiving in his bulging eyes. This man wears an ornate helmet of a sort medievalists classify as a

---

1   TCD Ms 1440.
2   TCD Ms 1440, f.18v.

GALLÓGLACH: PERSPECTIVES ON THE AXEMAN

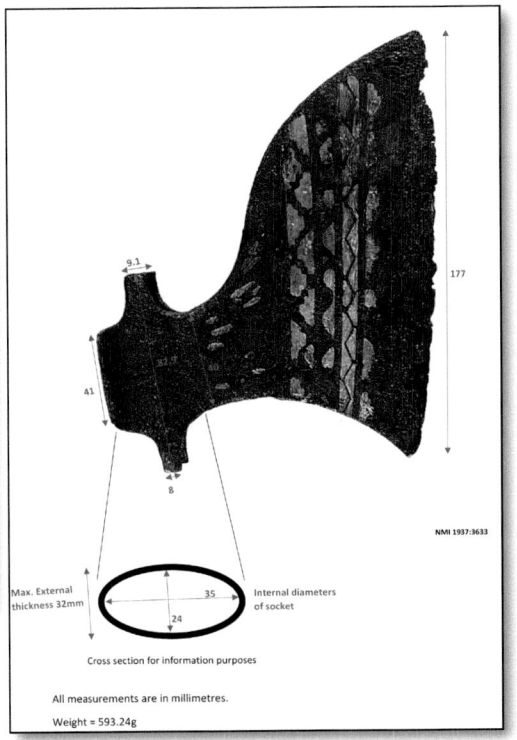

Battle-axe head with silver decoration in the National Museum of Ireland (object no. 1937:3633); possibly 14th or 15th century. (© National Museum of Ireland)

barbute or barbuta. The helmet is decorated in red and has a hook-shaped protrusion above the forehead, the hook being a well-known – but still unexplained – feature of Irish helmets.

The anonymous artist would have had access to the Bible, perhaps prints made by English or Continental artists, and memories of earlier artwork they had made and the art made by other craftspeople. Perhaps the artist used German prints for the scene's composition. The Bible does not describe how the Romans dressed, and the Roman soldiers here are not modelled on anything seen in a German print. Their mail armour, open-faced helmets, two-handed axes, domineering postures, severe faces, and the role they play as guardsmen, are the unmistakeable hallmarks of the 'galloglass,' from the Gaelic *gallóglach* (plural *gallóglaigh*). Perhaps the artist responsible for the de Burgos book got Íochtair's Mac Domhnaill (that is, MacDonnell or MacDonald) galloglass to pose as models.

Grim of Countenance

Galloglass were probably late medieval Ireland's most formidable soldiers, Stanihurst deeming them 'very powerful men and the foundation and strength of the Irish war machine.'[3] When galloglass have been examined by

---

3   Stanihurst, *Great Deeds*, p.123.

THE GAELIC WORLD AT WAR: SOLDIERS & SOLDIERING IN IRELAND 1366–1547

Figures of galloglass standing guard on the base of a tomb at Dungiven Priory, Co. Londonderry/Derry, for a member of the Ó Catháin (O'Cahan, O'Kane) family, who were lords of Keenaght. This galloglass has a gambeson, bascinet, spear and probably a sword. The tomb probably dates from about 1470–1500, but it is unclear which member of the Ó Catháin family it commemorates. (Artwork by Heather Cannan-Braniff)

historians, it is usually their family trees that have been studied, the details of their armament, training and systems of organisation being by and large overlooked.

Stanihurst may have rubbed shoulders with Irish soldiers when he was tutor to the children of the 11th Earl of Kildare at Rathangan Castle;[4] his pronouncement that galloglass were 'grim of countenance' certainly has a vivid clarity.[5] It sounds from this as though galloglass had a presence that went beyond physical strength and size. Shane Ó Néill's galloglass were similarly described as 'grim and redoubtable,'[6] but we need to think carefully about what is meant by 'grim.' Often quoting accounts like Stanihurst without explanation or context, historians have sensationalised galloglass, creating a false image of these elite fighters as maniacs whose military strength was innate and bestial rather than a product of experience and training.

For a start, there is every reason to believe that the 'grim' galloglass demeanour was probably a practised and performed attitude. We should also be aware of changes in word meaning. A grim countenance starts to take on a different meaning when we look at medieval accounts of what made a good commander. In her version of Vegetian theory, Christine de Pisan recommended that an army commander or 'Conestable' should be, to quote Caxton's late fifteenth century translation, 'Sadde in countenaunce' – 'sad' meaning in Caxton's time not merely unhappy, but sober and serious.[7]

Pisan's advice on what a commanding soldierly demeanour looked like was there for the taking if you were one of the Mac Domhnaill or Barrett galloglass stationed in or around Maynooth, given that the castle had a copy (though you might need to get an educated retainer to read it to you). Of course Stanihurst meant galloglass looked intimidating; just consider that cheery comment from Stanihurst that galloglass were haters of humanity and you get an idea

---

4   Barry & Morgan's introduction to Stanihurst, *Great Deeds*, p.4.
5   Stanihurst, *Irish Chronicle*, p.114.
6   Quoted in Hayes-McCoy, *Irish Battles*, p.76.
7   Christine de Pisan, *The Book of Fayttes of Armes and of Chyvalrye*, trans. William Caxton, ed. A. T. P. Byles (Early English Text Society & Kraus Reprint Co., 1971), pp.21–23.

of the impression these men made.[8] The very sound of the word 'galloglass' has a grimness to it, but we can start building a more accurate picture of galloglass if we understand them as intimidating because they emanated deadly serious professional dedication. In 1543 St Leger described to Henry VIII galloglass as the 'sorte of men [that] doo not lightly abandon the fielde,' but would face the 'brunte to the deathe.'[9]

Imagine, if you can, that ideal military leader described by Pisan – or a group of modern marines or paratroopers, or other professions which require physical authority, and to be calm and capable in a crisis – and then, arguably, you will have something of an accurate mental picture of the classic galloglass.

Galloglass: Origins and Definitions

Arriving from western Scotland, the galloglass spread through Ireland as they found work as mercenaries and bodyguards, recruiting Irishmen to fill out their ranks. The Irish-Scottish relationship worked because there was sufficient cultural affinity to mean there was an atmosphere of respect, familiarity and solidarity, with just enough difference between the two nations to mean that Scots brought something new to Irish armies. The

Rathmullan Castle in Donegal, also known as McSwine's Castle, photographed in the nineteenth century. (Courtesy of the University of St Andrews Libraries and Museums, ID: JV-3178).

---

8   One can understand why Edward MacLysaght, Ireland's chief herald in the mid-twentieth century, considered it unlikely that the MacSheehy family name of one of the galloglass dynasties, could mean 'peace'; '*sítheach*, eerie,' concluded MacLysaght, 'seems more probable' – E. MacLysaght, *The Surnames of Ireland* (Sallins: Irish Academic Press, 2023, 6th edn), p.270.

9   Quoted in Lydon, 'Scottish Soldier Abroad,' in Duffy, *Robert the Bruce's Irish Wars*, p.106.

new quality Scots brought to Irish armies was a greater emphasis on the value of heavy infantry. Irish noblemen had always had access to armour and heavy hand weapons, but the concept of tightly disciplined units of heavy infantry, often using two-handed weapons, was a Scottish speciality.

In addition to units of galloglass, it appears chiefs (and some English officials) retained a single galloglass as their *gallóglach tighearna* ('lord's galloglass'), which seems to have meant a personal bodyguard (and possibly champion).[10] While it is common sense for leaders to have bodyguards, the concept of heavy infantry guardsmen can be traced to two specific traditions: the medieval Scottish preference for heavy infantry fighting, and the old Scandinavian custom of elite household bodyguards. Many galloglass came from the Scottish isles where Scandinavian military traditions remained strong, and, indeed, there is perhaps something of an Elizabethan galloglass in the appearance of the burgonet-wearing, axe-bearing, moustachioed 'Dane' who guards the frontispiece of John Speed's early seventeenth century map-book of Britain and Ireland.[11]

The Galloglass Axe: Symbol

Galloglass were almost always thought of as axe-armed heavy infantry, the definition given in the English 1597 survey of MacCarthy Mór's territories being typical: '*Gallogoloh* were a certayne companye of foote soldiers beringe axes.'[12] Or, according to a 1587 glossary of Desmond rents, '*Galloglas*' were a 'nomb[er]of soldiers, to put the contrie to charge [i.e. the local community had the burden of providing them with housing and sustenance], bearinge axes.'[13] The galloglass leadership themselves likely considered the axe their signature weapon, since axes feature prominently in the coats of arms that they adopted at the end of the Middle Ages.[14]

Guardsmen through history have often been armed with axes because axes are good weapons, and because axes have strong connotations of judicial, civic and regal power. Early modern Dublin had the 'Battle-Axe

---

10 K. Nicholls, 'Scottish Mercenary Kindreds in Ireland, 1200–1600,' in Duffy, *World of the Galloglass*, pp.86–87.

11 England inherited some of the same Scandinavian traditions, giving rise to the *huscarle* and *hearthweru* or 'hearth-guard.' Alexander Richey, a QC and historian born in Dublin in 1830, saw this, saying in his *Short History of the Irish People* (Dublin: Hodges, Figgis and Co., 1887), p.17, that the 'gallowglass in Ireland was the equivalent of the "housecarl" in England.'

12 'The Desmond Survey,' published online at CELT.

13 Hore & Graves, *Social State*, p.266.

14 Cannan, 'Machiavellian Mercenaries?' Axes do not, in contrast, feature in the arms of the kern-leading Purcells (who, appropriately for kern, have a sword in their crest) or Keatings (whose bellicosity is amply conveyed in their coat of arms by four nettles on their shield, together with a fifth in their crest which is represented as being chewed by a boar!)

GALLÓGLACH: PERSPECTIVES ON THE AXEMAN

Guard,' and an area of the city's castle is known as the 'Battle-Axe Landing.' The Latin *securis* means both 'axe' and 'authority,' and no doubt because *securiger* ('armed with an axe') resembles *securitas* ('security'), axes drop in and out of translations of William Camden's oft-quoted description of the galloglass who came with Shane O'Neill to London in 1562. But Camden does mention axes in his Latin first edition published in 1615: '*Shanus O-Neal* … cum securigero *Galloglassorum* satellitio' (= 'Shane O'Neill … with a bodyguard of axe-armed galloglass'). Nor can we allow the sanitising of Camden's description of galloglass shirts to escape uncorrected. Modern history books include Camden's remark that the galloglass wore shirts that were saffron-coloured, and seem unaware of what Camden says in the

From the reign of Charles II until 1832 the Battle-Axe Guard garrisoned Dublin Castle. Battle-Axe Guardsmen can be seen standing on the bottom right of this painting, made in 1731 by the Dutch artist, William van der Hagen, of a state ball at Dublin Castle. Joseph Cooper Walker, a Dublin-born antiquary who died in 1810, considered these ceremonial guardsmen as heirs to the galloglass. Despite the name of the formation, the Battle-Axe Guard carried 'partisans' and they did not, in costume or social composition, in any way resemble galloglass, being obviously modelled on the English Yeomen of the Guard. However, Walker was not wrong, for over the generations the galloglass had clearly entered deep enough into the psyche of Irish officials for a unit of Dublin guardsmen to be named after the galloglass' hallmark weapon. (Private Collection)

original Latin about the galloglass shirts – namely, that they were the colour of infected or diseased human urine![15]

The Galloglass Axe: Weapon

There are no galloglass fighting-technique manuals, since we are dealing with an age when orality and memory were commonly accepted ways for important information to be preserved; after all, no Englishman appears to have written a treatise on archery until the 1500s.[16] Nonetheless, one wonders whether a galloglass would have recognised some of the poll-axe moves in the *Fechtbuch* ('Fight Book') of the fifteenth century German weapons-master Hans Talhoffer. Talhoffer's illustrations show how versatile the two-handed axe or pollaxe is, and how in trained hands the haft, as well as the blade, is a weapon.[17] Axe-fighting was almost as much about staff-fighting – itself a martial art – as cutting with the blade.

Cormac Bourke has cautioned against calling surviving axe-heads 'galloglass axes' just because they look the part, as other warriors might have used the same type of axe.[18] Wiser is the antiquary who calls such objects 'axes of galloglass type,' or a 'galloglass-type axe,' and who comprehends that we appear to be dealing with a distinct Irish (and probably west Scottish) style of axe that galloglass used, as opposed to a style of axe unique to galloglass. Sir Guy Laking, one of the most famous historians of arms and armour, felt Irish and Welsh 'armaments' had 'no great racial characteristic,' being generally 'crude' and without 'artistic individuality.'[19] But, surely, what is so arresting about galloglass-type axes is that, like Irish ring-pommel swords and traditional Irish *scian* daggers, they can be *very* strongly distinctive.[20]

The Class 21 Axe

But, to be clear, it is one style of axe used by the galloglass that is distinctive – the type Cormac Bourke classified as the 'Class 21' axe head:

---

15 William Camden, *Annales* (London, 1615), vol. 1, p.78: 'humana vrina infectis'.
16 C. Bartlett, *English Longbowman 1330–1515* (Oxford: Osprey, 2020), p.4.
17 Hans Talhoffer (M. Rector, trans. & ed.), *Medieval Combat: A Fifteenth-Century Illustrated Manual of Swordfighting and Close-Quarter Combat* (London: Greenhill, 2000), plates 79–103.
18 In discussion with the author, 2005.
19 G. F. Laking, *A Record of European Armour and Arms Through Seven Centuries* (Milton Keynes: Benediction Classics, 2009), vol. 5, p.55.
20 For the *scian* or *skean*, see R. Gresh, *The Skean: The Distinctive Fighting Knife of Gaelic Ireland 1500–1700* (Atglen, PA: Schiffer, 2023).

GALLÓGLACH: PERSPECTIVES ON THE AXEMAN

...the upper edge is convex and the lower edge is concave. The blade is elongated and the straight cutting edge is vertical or divergent from the line of the haft. .... The shaft-hole is of rounded, pointed-oval or lozenge-shaped form.[21]

The dating of galloglass-type axe-heads is, however, problematic. There is often little basis for the dates that have been assigned to such axe-heads ('sixteenth century' being a popular label imposed on these axes by historians). 'Late medieval' is often the best we can do. At the same time, the halberd-style Class 21 axe may have been a fifteenth century innovation. Perhaps the earliest dateable representation of a Class 21 axe head is a carved stone panel of the Resurrection at Ennis, Co. Clare, which was erected around 1470 by More Ni Brien (and reused in the nineteenth century as a tomb for Creaghs of Dangan).[22] In the Ennis Resurrection panel, a Roman soldier is portrayed very much as the quintessential galloglass with bascinet and Class 21 axe. It was during this period – the late Middle Ages and the Renaissance – that pollaxes and halberds were widespread in England and Europe, and it may be that the halberd Class 21 style of galloglass axe appeared in the later fifteenth century.

The three other galloglass 'legionaries' in the Ennis Resurrection panel are armed with a spear and traditional crescent-shaped battleaxes, however. This could be because the older crescent-shaped axe – Bourke's Class 11 – [23]

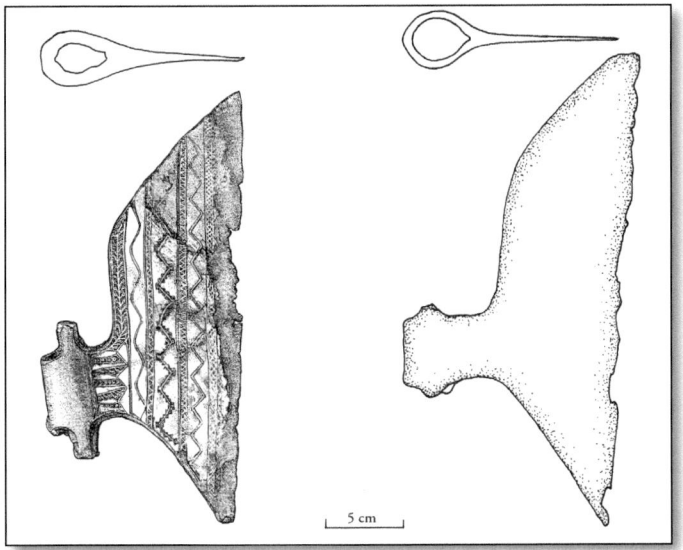

Two 'Class 21' axe-heads, found during dredging of the Blackwater River, and now in the Ulster Museum. Very tentatively, we can suggest that they date from the period c. 1450–c. 1600. The axe on the left (UM object no. A78.1990) was found in the Blackwater within Clonteevy townland, Co. Tyrone, and is decorated with silver foil. Length of blade's cutting edge (measured vertically): 29.1cm; width (measured horizontally): 13.5cm; shaft-hole internal measurements: 3 x 1.9cm; weight: 831.7gms. The right-hand axe (object no. RS1999.51) was found in the Blackwater within Derryloughan townland, Co. Tyrone. Length of blade's cutting edge (measured vertically): 31.2cm; width (measured horizontally): 15.4cm; shaft-hole internal measurements: 3.7cm x 3.1cm; weight, 549.1gms. (Reproduced from C. Bourke's 2001 article on axe-heads from the Blackwater)

---

21 C. Bourke, 'Antiquities from the River Blackwater III, Iron Axe-Heads' in *Ulster Journal of Archaeology*, 3rd series, 60 (2001), p.64.
22 F. Cannan, 'Holy Images from England: Medieval English Alabaster Sculpture in Ireland' in *History Ireland*, vol. 22, no. 1 (Jan./Feb. 2014), p.18.
23 Bourke, 'Antiquities from the River Blackwater', p. 64.

was still being used by galloglass (a galloglass in the sixteenth century 'Book of the de Burgos' carries one) or simply because Class 11s are a much easier shape to draw, paint or sculpt than Class 21s.

Examining surviving Class 21 axe-heads, one again wonders if their design was inspired by European halberds or pollaxes from the end of the Middle Ages. The Ulster Museum (UM) has three Class 21 axe-heads (four if what appears to be a fragment of a Class 21 axe is included) which were found during dredging of the Blackwater river in Cos. Armagh and Tyrone between 1984 and 1991.[24] Found in an area where Ó Neill's Mac Domhnaill galloglass operated (if only these objects could speak!), the three axe-heads have cutting edges around 30cm long,[25] which matches with Stanihurst's remark that the blades on galloglass axes were 'one foot long.'[26] The three Blackwater axes are not heavy; two weigh just half a kilo.[27] The heaviest of the three, a silver-decorated weapon (museum no. A78.1990), is still less than a kilo.[28] Another Class 21 weapon, a silver-decorated axe head in the National Museum of Ireland (object no. 1937:3633), weighs a little over half a kilo.[29]

In other words, it would be wrong to imagine (as many do) that it was sheer size and weight that did the damage. These are weapons to be wielded with nimbleness and skill. Not all galloglass-style axe-heads are particularly large. The National Museum of Ireland's silver-decorated axe head (NMI 1937:3633) belongs within Class 21 but may be earlier (perhaps fourteenth or fifteenth century) than the Ulster Museum's Class 21 axe-heads dredged from the Blackwater (which are probably *c*. 1450–*c*. 1600). All we have by way of provenance for NMI 1937:3633 is that it is said to have been found in 1910 in Donegal (so could it have belonged to a Mac Suibhne…?) and formed part of the Swan collection.[30] It is decorated with silver arranged into 'step and zigzag' patterns which, as R. Ó Floinn observed, look early, perhaps even twelfth century.[31] Instead it may well be that Irish arms-makers continued to use old styles of decoration on new shapes of axes, since the axe head's shape looks late medieval. On the other hand, the shape of the axe head is less decidedly halberd than the Ulster Museum examples

---

24 Axe nos. 124, 125, 126 (and probably 127) in Bourke, 'Antiquities from the River Blackwater'.
25 Bourke, 'Antiquities from the River Blackwater,' pp.68, 82–83.
26 Stanihurst, *Great Deeds*, p.123.
27 Bourke, 'Antiquities from the River Blackwater,' p.68. From the weight of what survives (341.2 gms), it looks like the fourth Class 21 axe head from the Blackwater would have weighed about the same, i.e. half or just over half a kilo (*ibid.*, pp.68, 83).
28 'Antiquities from the River Blackwater,' p.68.
29 My thanks for this information from NMI staff.
30 Information again supplied by NMI staff; also R. Ó Floinn, 'Sandhills, Silver and Shrines – Fine Metalwork of the Medieval Period from Donegal,' in Nolan, Ronayne & Dunlevy, *Donegal*, p.99.
31 Ó Floinn, 'Sandhills,' in Nolan, Ronayne & Dunlevy, *Donegal*, p.99.

GALLÓGLACH: PERSPECTIVES ON THE AXEMAN

from the Blackwater, and still a little more 'Dane axe', suggesting this could be an older weapon than those found in the Blackwater.

NMI 1937:3633 is also surprisingly petite – if, that is, it was designed to be attached to a handle as long as those used by galloglass.[32] In 2023, I commissioned Tim Noyes of Heron Armouries, Kent, to make a galloglass axe based on NMI 1937:3633, but with differing silver, bronze and brass decoration. Noyes wedged the finished axe head with English oak to a six-foot ash pole ('six foote longe' being John Dymmok's description of galloglass axes).[33] The finished axe is a light, lively weapon. The relative smallness of its head is suggestive of precise, well-aimed blows rather than crazed hacking. The overall style and handling of the weapon feels more like an English man-at-arms' pollaxe from the period of Bosworth than a 'Dane axe'.[34]

Decoration

Both heavily decorated with silver, UM A78.1990 and NMI 1937:3633 are probably the two finest surviving galloglass-type weapons. It is undeniable that the decoration is simple compared to the best weapons produced in Germany and Italy, but if the impression one gets is not of immense technical skill, it is one of dependability, durability and fearsome cleaving power. As for adornment, were some galloglass axe handles decorated? The haft of the finished Noyes axe was painted and decorated by the author in medieval maximalist style on the basis that European medieval

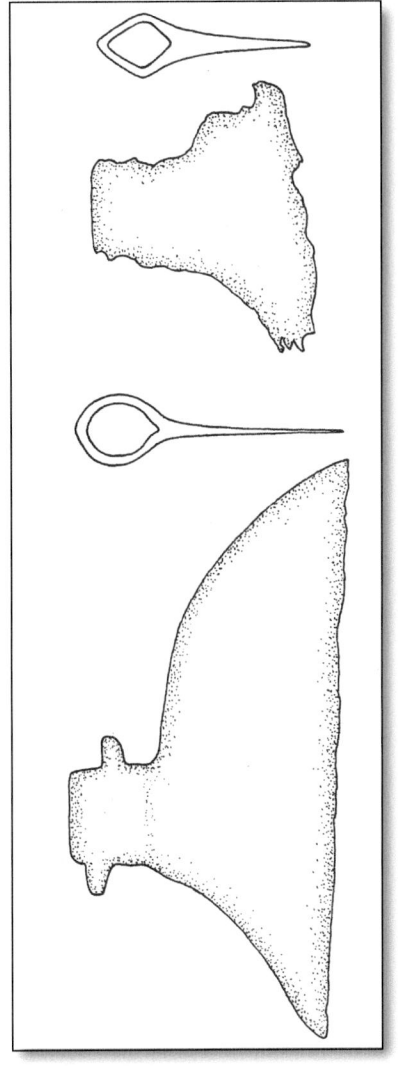

Two more Class 21 axe-heads found during dredging of the Blackwater. Both may date from c. 1450–c. 1600, and both are now in the Ulster Museum. The bottom axe (UM object no. RS1992.134) was found within Annaghbeg townland, Co. Tyrone. Length of blade's cutting edge (measured vertically): 30.5cm; width (measured horizontally), 14cm; shaft-hole internal measurements: 3.7cm x 2.6cm; weight, 493.1gms. The fragment of an axe illustrated at top (UM object no. RS1999.67) was found in Derryloughan townland, Co. Tyrone. Width (measured horizontally): 11.8cm; shaft-hole internal measurements: 3.3cm x 2.6cm; weight, 341.2gms. (reproduced from C. Bourke's 2001 article on axe-heads from the Blackwater)

---

32 Could galloglass-type axe-heads have been sometimes mounted on short hafts and used as single-handed weapons?
33 Dymmok, *Treatice*, p.7.
34 The blade (length: 17.7cm) on NMI 1937:3633 (and subsequent Noyes copy) is a very similar in length to two fifteenth century Wallace Collection pollaxes (A925, blade length 15.3cm; A926, blade length 19cm). Measurements from J. Mann, *European Arms and Armour* (London & Beccles: Wallace Collection catalogue, 1962), vol. 2: *Arms*, pp.2441–2442.

THE GAELIC WORLD AT WAR: SOLDIERS & SOLDIERING IN IRELAND 1366-1547

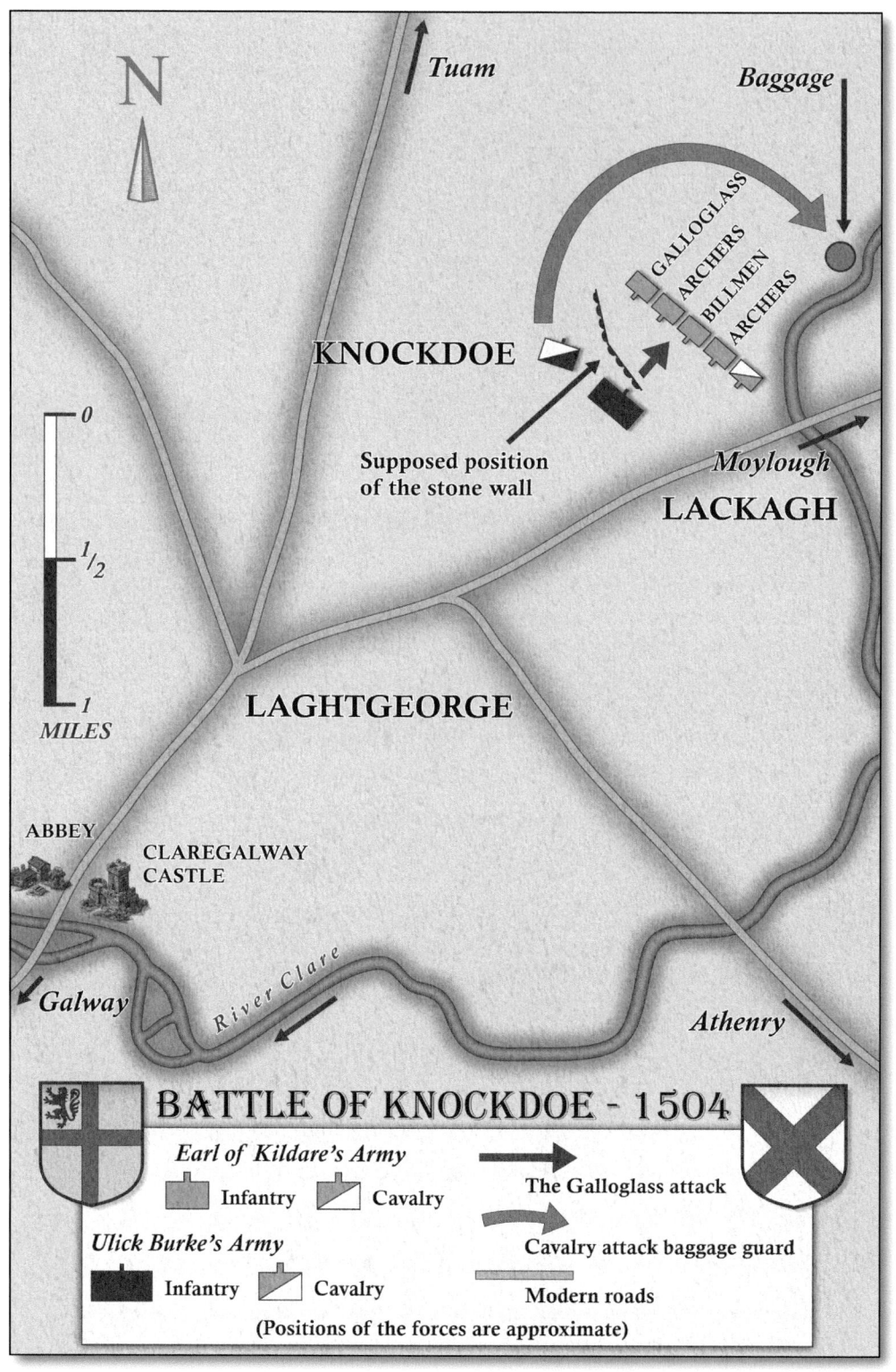

Positioning according to G.A. Hayes-McCoy of forces at the battle of Knockdoe, fought on 19th August 1504, to the north-east of Galway town (now Galway city). Galloglass were a decisive feature of the battle.

tastes were not minimalist, and that there is nothing to indicate Gaeldom differed from the medieval cultural 'mainstream' in this regard.

The shaft of the weapon wielded by Art Mór Mac Murchadha, who had revived the title of King of Leinster, is shown decorated with stripes in Jean Creton's manuscript history of the deposing of Richard II.[35] This picture has been reproduced a number of times but few appreciate its significance as an artwork based on eyewitness testimony rather than hearsay. Creton had accompanied Richard to Ireland in 1399 and saw Mac Murchadha ride down from the hills to negotiate with the English army.[36] Creton describes precisely what can be seen in the Harley Ms illustration, how Mac Murchadha galloped down a steep slope through a gap between two woods at great speed towards the English, and how in 'his right hand he bore a great long dart, which he cast with much skill.'[37] One wonders if Creton had advised the artist on these details, including perhaps the dress and physical appearance of Mac Murchadha and his followers.

Doubtless much of the tassels, paintwork, stud work and so forth on weaponry was a mere show of wealth. Some of it probably had a religious significance. Some decoration, though, may have signified authority, if only because such decoration was expensive. A critical 'Information' compiled 'Anno 1541' about Leonard Grey's time as chief governor or 'Lord Deputy' of Ireland includes an intriguing reference to a lone 'Gallowglasse wt a silver sparre or Ax, and the hilt therof hanginge full of silke' acting as a 'guide' for Grey and his men, 'and so went wt them to Gallway.'[38] Did this decorated axe – sometimes called a 'spar' in Ireland, the word being also applied to a galloglass and his attendants – show the man's authority (or authority to act on behalf of superiors), similar to the tasselled, ornate polearms carried by early modern army officers and NCOs? After all, it is said there were sergeants in the Desmond lands, albeit possibly acting as civil officials.

Galloglass Axes: Manufacture & Value

Given the distinctiveness of the Class 21 axe, and the power and skill represented by the *gallóglach* axe, especially a decorated one, it is no surprise that they were taken as trophies by the English. In an account published in 1580, John Hooker described Sir Peter Carew (cousin of George) in action in Ireland 11 years earlier:

> …they were advertised by their scouts and espials, that all, or the most part of the galloglasses of Sir Edmund Butler lay in a certain place about two or three miles out of Kilkenny: whereupon Sir Peter,

---

35   British Library Harley Ms 1319, f.9.
36   McGettigan, *Richard II*, p.176.
37   Quoted in McGettigan, *Richard II*, p.176.
38   Lambeth Palace, Carew Ms 601 ff.35, 38r.

assembling all his captains and company, concluded to issue out and to give the onset upon them… and gave an utter overthrown to the enemy, being in number about two hundred, few or none of them being escaped unkilled … When the fight was ended and the enemies overthrown, every man took a gallowglass axe of theirs who were slain, and carried with them into the town in sign of victory.[39]

One imagines that, once settled in Ireland, galloglass used local Irish smiths to make their axes, although it may well be that Highland-made axes were transported over now and then. There is nothing particularly complex about the construction of the UM and NMI's galloglass-like axe-heads. Although they do not have maker's marks, they very much resemble the kind of rugged, functional weaponry which we know was made by Gaelic armourer-smiths.[40] Irish armourers have received almost no attention from scholars,[41] but they appear to have had much in common with those of the Scottish Highlands and Islands where armourer-smiths had a high status (indeed sometimes noble status), were often part of a chief's retinue, often worked on a hereditary basis, and appear to have been more all-round metalworkers than specialists.[42]

There were no large arms workshops in Gaelic Ireland or Scotland, so we should conjure in our mind's eye an image of skilled cottage industries repairing, fixing, adapting and making everything the local soldiers required, and working flat out in the run up to hostilities. In 1589 it was reported that the Mac Domhnaill galloglass of Mayo had 'made of late 400 gallowglass axes' and 'daily they are making Gallowglass axes, and other weapons.'[43] That galloglass axes were usually straightforward pieces to make is suggested by the modest monetary value assigned to a galloglass axe in a 1596 'Inventorie' of all the 'goodes

Axe on six-foot ash haft (with oak wedge) made for the author by Tim Noyes of Heron Armouries, Kent. The axe head bears the Cannan cross in bronze, silver and brass. The painted decoration and tassel on the haft are by Fergus Cannan. (Author's Photograph)

39   John Hooker (J. Maclean, ed.) *The Life and Times of Sir Peter Carew, Kt* (London, 1857), pp.94–95.
40   F. Cannan, 'A Family of Highland Blacksmiths: The Macnabs of Barachastlain' in *Journal of the Antique Metalware Society*, vol. 19 (2011), pp.30–37; F. Cannan, 'The "Clanranald Anvil"' in *Journal of the Antique Metalware Society*, vol. 21 (2013), pp.50–57; F. Cannan, *Scottish Arms and Armour* (Oxford: Shire, 2009), chap. 3.
41   Although see B.G. Scott's groundbreaking *Early Irish Ironworking* (Ulster Museum Publication No. 266).
42   See Cannan, 'Family of Highland Blacksmiths; Cannan, '"Clanranald Anvil"'; Cannan, *Scottish Arms and Armour*, chap. 3.
43   Quoted in G. A. Hayes-McCoy, 'The Gallóglach Axe' in *Journal of the Galway Archaeological and Historical Society*, 17 (1937), p.112.

and cattelles of the late reverend father in God Hugh Bushoppe of Chester.' In 'ye ward roobe' the bishop had 'a gally glasse axe' valued by the makers of the inventory at 'ijs' (2 shillings).[44] The bishop in question was Hugh Bellot (1542–1596), Bishop of Chester and Bangor, but it is not known why he had a galloglass axe! Bellot had an interest in the Welsh language,[45] so perhaps his interest in 'Celtic' matters extended to Ireland. Nor is it far from Wales and Chester to Ireland. Kern working for the Crown were in Chester in 1550; maybe one of them sold his axe or it was a diplomatic gift.[46]

Unless this was a damaged high-class weapon, a 2-shilling axe would likely be a basic combat item produced for an ordinary galloglass, perhaps to be stored in a constable's arsenal. By way of comparison, two halberds with red silk fringes are valued in the 1596 inventory of the Bishop of Chester's possessions at 10 shillings for the pair, and two plain halberds at 5 shillings the pair.[47] To put this in context, in England in 1597 half a dozen pigeons cost 2 shillings, while in Ireland in 1588, Henry Duke, 'General of her Majesty's kerne,' was paid 2s 8d per day, while his 30 kern each received 4d per day.[48] In 1562, it appears a group of galloglass were paid 8d per day.[49] Like the English shilling, an Irish shilling was 12 pence. English and Irish currency had slightly different values, but we can estimate that Bishop Hugh's axe was worth something like three or four days' pay for a galloglass, or at least 6 days' pay for one of Henry Duke's kern.

Athletic All-Rounders

Talhoffer's book shows that the killer blow is dealt at the precise moment when your opponent is vulnerable and all the conditions are right. Only amateurs slash away; the expert fighter is creative and resourceful, using every part of the weapon to attack and parry. So are we to take seriously the illustration in Derricke's *Image of Irelande* showing galloglass swinging their axes above their heads with both hands as they attempt to hold back English halberdiers?[50] Unless your opponent is pretty much beaten, this posture leaves you dangerously exposed, and jars with the wisdom of Talhoffer. One way of interpreting this posture is to see it as a terror tactic,

---

44 G. J. Piccope (ed.), *Lancashire and Cheshire Wills and Inventories from the Ecclesiastical Court, Chester*, (Manchester: The Chetham Society, 1861), 3rd portion, pp.1–4.
45 'Bellot, Hugh,' *ODNB* (entry by G. Williams).
46 *OED*, 'Kern' (under the year 1550).
47 *Lancashire and Cheshire Wills*, p.4.
48 List of army wages for 1588 in Carew Ms 625, f.1.
49 Hayes-McCoy, *Scots Mercenary Forces*, p.60.
50 The same pose can be seen in an image from the period of the Hundred Years' War of a stern-looking soldier who rather resembles a galloglass (he wears a bascinet and quilted jacket), standing bolt upright on a bridge, axe raised above his head with both hands.

THE GAELIC WORLD AT WAR: SOLDIERS & SOLDIERING IN IRELAND 1366–1547

Illustration based on old photographs, written accounts and the ruins themselves, of Barachastlain where the Macnabs, a family of Highland armourer-smiths, worked for several centuries. Like many of the hereditary smiths of Scotland and Ireland, the Macnabs had, and still have, a high status in the retinue of their chief. (Drawing by F. Cannan -Braniff)

the warrior knowing it leaves them vulnerable – but only if their opponents have the guts to come forward and engage.

But while there is always a strong psychological component to single-handed combat, determination and aggression are not by themselves enough. The ultimate galloglass may have been a big man, but he would not have lasted long if he was lumbering and without skill. To fight like the people in Talhoffer's pictures takes training, cardio-vascular fitness and to be light on your feet. As any reenactor who has fought on wet grass or smooth paving slabs will tell you, medieval footwear did not have terrific grip – but medieval shoes are not so bad if you can be light-footed and use the balls of your feet. This (rather than poverty) is why some Gaelic Scots and Irish fought barefoot. So, surely, we should think of a skilled Gaelic warrior as fighting like a light-footed samurai, moving, parrying and blocking – and with a range of weapons, not exclusively the axe.

Galloglass would not have been in such demand if they had only been adept at heavy axe-fighting on the battlefield as most Irish warfare did not consist of pitched battles. Much more common in Ireland, and elsewhere in medieval Europe, was raiding, harrying and assassination. A two-handed axe is not a good weapon for hit-and-run raids, and there is no need to see galloglass as always using this weapon.

The pair of warriors on the left of Dürer's 1521 representation of 'Irishmen' has a ring of accuracy about it: one has a double-handed sword, the other a spear. This looks like a 'buddy' or tag-team system, where, supported by their servants, the two men will act as their own small unit, the spearman clearing away any opponents getting too close, guarding the flanks, thus allowing the two-handed sword (actually a weapon more associated, as far as we know, with Highlanders than galloglass) to go to work.[51] Without defence from spears, javelins, swords and other fast weapons, the two-handed sword or axe can quickly become vulnerable to rush attacks, or attacks from behind. This does not mean Dürer saw real Irishmen, only that he has created an accurate illustration of how late medieval/renaissance soldiers used two-handed weapons.

John Dymmok, a late Tudor writer about whom we know nothing, but who writes like someone with a sound understanding of Irish military matters, actually says that the 'batle axe, or halberd' was the weapon galloglass 'most vse,' not exclusively use.[52] Spears as well as axes are thus shown in the de Burgos representation of galloglass. Dymmok also says 'a skeine' (*scian*) was part of the galloglass' typical equipment.[53] There is evidence for use of javelins by galloglass (good at unnerving and disordering the enemy),[54] and swords, which are a status symbol, even if fairly ineffective against heavy armour.[55]

Given that pitched battles were not everyday occurrences, it is likely Irish chiefs hired galloglass because galloglass were good all-round soldiers able to fight in a variety of scenarios with a variety of weapons, and, it appears, to fight unarmed with their bodies. Galloglass had to be good because there was plenty of competition in the mercenary trade from new

---

51 No one has pursued the possibility that these 'Irishmen' may actually be Highlanders (who were often referred to as 'Irish'). There is no evidence for galloglass use of two-handed swords other than Dürer's 1521 image. But galloglass would not have had a problem fighting with a two-handed sword and re-enactors perhaps limit their use to recreations of non-rank-and-file galloglass (e.g. a galloglass constable or lord's galloglass) and be aware that they are moving into more speculative, imaginative territory.

52 Dymmok, *Treatice*, p.7. It has been suggested that Dymmok may have served with the Earl of Essex in Ireland at the close of the 1500s. Dymmok dedicates the 'rude leaves' of his *Treatice of Ireland* to 'Sir Edmude Carye' – presumably the Sir Edmund Carey who commanded Elizabeth I's bodyguard during the Armada campaign, and was a cousin of the Queen: see History of Parliament Online, 'Carey, Sir Edmund.' Could Dymmok have been the late sixteenth century John Dymock who appears on a Welsh family tree as the son of Thomas Dymock de Halchton in Flintshire, and Jenet, sister and heiress of John ap Owen Puleston? See Samuel Rush Meyrick (ed.), *Heraldic Visitations of Wales and Part of the Marches* (Llandovery: William Rees, 1846), vol. 2, p.314. Or perhaps Dymmok was a scion of the famous Dymoke family of Scrivelsby in Lincolnshire, hereditary champions to the monarchs of England?

53 Dymmok, *Treatice*, p.7.

54 Two galloglass are shown throwing javelins to cover the retreat of their unit in one of the illustrations in Derricke's *Image of Irelande*.

55 Figures of galloglass with swords guard the base of the Felim O'Connor or Ó Conchobhair's late fifteenth century tomb at Roscommon abbey. James Ware's *Antiquities and History of Ireland* (Dublin: A. Crook, 1705), p.31, says galloglass were armed with both swords and axes.

Command & Control

The suggestion that there might have been galloglass insignia to indicate seniority may jar with readers conditioned by the old belief that Gaelic armies were unruly gatherings capable only of brawls and wild charges. Yet systems were in place for the command and control of Gaelic soldiers. Two youthful-looking individuals wearing stylish lined hats, mail and hose, and riding smartly harnessed horses, are shown acting with some authority in the depiction of Christ carrying the cross from the 'Book of the de Burgos'. One gestures with a sceptre or mace, conceivably symbolising his status as a senior officer in the Burke household. Perhaps he is even a very young marshal or constable in Burke's private army.

Gaelic armies had banners, musicians and battle-cries to assist with rallying and maintaining cohesion. Art Ó Gallchobhair, Bishop of Raphoe, came from an old Donegal military dynasty and was remembered after his death in 1561 as always travelling with a 'troupe of Horsemen under his collours.'[56] It is on record, too, that in 1534 Gerald 'Boye' Prendergast and others led 1,000 men 'with a banner displayed' to burn Balmagir in Wexford.[57] Again, it is recorded that in the '19th yeare' of Henry VIII's reign a Kavanagh force 'with banner displayed' raided in and around Wexford town, aided by a David Keating.[58]

Displaying one's banner meant hostilities had commenced and was a declaration of one's right to wage private war. There is no evidence for marching or troop movement in time with music, though; medieval Gaelic use of banners appears limited to using them as rallying points and as symbols of unit, dynastic or regional honour. Taking another warrior's banner was therefore a tremendous sign of triumph, and Loutfut stressed a commander should choose their 'bannerman' carefully as they had to be especially 'strang,' loyal and 'expert in armis.'[59] When, indeed, Maol Mhuire Mac Suibhne of Fanad was killed fighting the Ó Néills in 1472, his body was taken to Derry covered in a Mac Domhnaill flag captured in the same battle.[60]

There were also more mystical means of instilling feelings of unity and confidence among soldiers, such as the 'armour and stone of St Columbkille' mentioned in a document in the Royal Irish Academy entitled

---

56   Quoted in J. J. Silke, 'Raphoe and the Reformation,' in Nolan, Ronayne & Dunlevy, *Donegal*, p.267.
57   Hore & Graves, *Social State*, p.43.
58   Hore & Graves, *Social State*, p.50.
59   Quoted in Allmand, *The De Re Militari*, p.236.
60   Gillespie, 'Gaelic Families,' in Nolan, Ronayne & Dunlevy, *Donegal*, p.781.

'the Will of Donall O'Gallagher aged 41 years concerning all the old customs of O'Donnell in the territory of Tirconnell A.D. 1626.'[61] The original seventeenth century document seems to be lost but a translation from Irish made in the nineteenth century by one of the greatest of all Gaelic historians, John O'Donovan, tells how the Boghaineach or Banagh Mac Suibhne sept provided their lord, Ó Domhnaill, with '60 gallowglasses' and 'a person' to carry Columcille's armour and stone.[62] St Colum Cille (or Columcille, Columkille, Columba) is one of Ireland's most revered saints, and it is likely that this stone was a well-known charm believed to work miracles known as 'An Cloch Ruadh' ('The Red Stone').[63] As for the armour, it is possible it was a piece of mail that was believed to have belonged to Colum Cille, and that the two objects were borne by a cleric of the Ó Náthan (O'Nahan/Nawn) family, perhaps in oath-swearing ceremonies or ritual blessings before combat.[64]

But if holy objects might supercharge the atmosphere in an army, sending a feeling of supernatural confidence around the ranks, it was also believed that God expected earthly leaders to plan sensibly and act rationally by appointing competent military commanders. Pisan's use of the term 'constable' is of direct relevance to galloglass, since the title was used by galloglass commanders (a point we will return to). Although authority always derived principally from social status in Irish armies, the records suggest a more formalised hierarchy was followed in galloglass units, in which it will be seen that each galloglass was in effect commander of his own little sub-unit of one or two assistants, perhaps resembling the following hierarchy:

No medieval banners appear to survive in Ireland, and there cannot be many older than this one. This painted banner has been preserved in a heraldic register kept by the Irish heralds for the years 1698–1800, and is now in the National Library of Ireland. Banners were used in the medieval and early modern periods to keep troops in formation during battle. Raising one's banner was a signal that war had broken out or that one had taken control of an area. Banners were also a key part of funeral rites to commemorate deceased nobles, and it is possible that this banner was made for funerary purposes. (Image from Grants and Confirmations of Arms, vol. A: 1698–1800; reproduced courtesy of the National Library of Ireland)

---

61 RIA Miscellaneous O'Donovan MS 14/B/7, p.423.
62 RIA Miscellaneous O'Donovan MS 14/B/7, p.423.
63 See Cannan, 'Machiavellian Mercenaries?'
64 See Cannan, 'Machiavellian Mercenaries?'

THE GAELIC WORLD AT WAR: SOLDIERS & SOLDIERING IN IRELAND 1366–1547

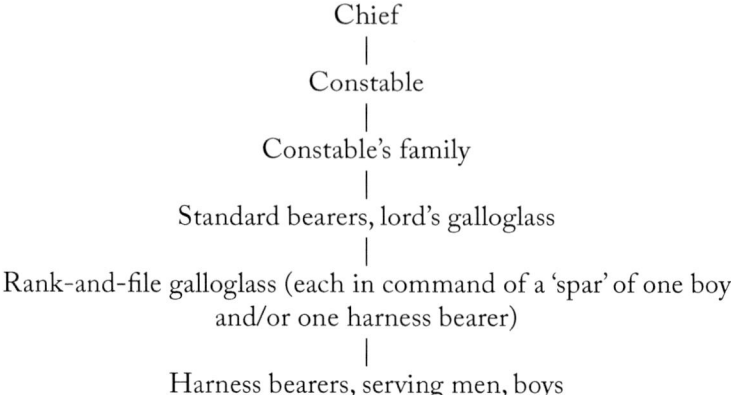

Chief
|
Constable
|
Constable's family
|
Standard bearers, lord's galloglass
|
Rank-and-file galloglass (each in command of a 'spar' of one boy and/or one harness bearer)
|
Harness bearers, serving men, boys

Household Servitors or Landed Gentry?

In one of his enthusiastic letters written as he explored the north of Ireland for the Ordnance Survey in the summer of 1835, John O'Donovan hailed the Mac Suibhnes of Fanad, Co. Donegal, as 'distinguished gentlemen of war,'[65] and it is certainly true that the Mac Suibhne galloglass were very eminent. But here we encounter another issue with the way galloglass are perceived by modern historians, for it is all too easy to imagine a galloglass chief as a kind of captain of the household guard, participating in watch duties in the great hall, axe in hand just like his soldiers. This is probably accurate if the galloglass leader was just starting out and yet to make a name for themselves – perhaps like the Barrett who commanded 24 galloglass for the Earl of Kildare in the late 1400s.[66]

Otherwise it is too humble a picture. Once settled in Ireland, galloglass constables began recruiting Irishmen. By about the end of the fifteenth century, the majority of the men in a galloglass unit would have been Irishmen. Many of the men serving in a Mac Domhnaill galloglass contingent had typically Mayo surnames,[67] and the men in a Mac Suibhne galloglass unit in Connacht in the 1580s again appear to have Irish names.[68] A 1573 pardon issued to members of the Mac Domhnaill galloglass family of Tinnakill lists two pipers and many Irishmen; possibly they were only the Mac Domhnaills' servants or tenants, but it is just as likely they were

---

65 Letter from O'Donovan dated 31 August 1835: RIA 14/C/11/9, p.5.
66 F. Cannan, 'If the Father Hath Been a Galloglass…', *Family History Monthly*, issue 180 (March 2010), p.36.
67 K. Nicholls, *Gaelic and Gaelicized Ireland* (Dublin: Lilliput Press, 2003, 2nd edn), p.102.
68 Hayes-McCoy, *Scots Mercenary Forces*, p.71.

Mac Domhnaill rank-and-file galloglass (or military followers of some sort, perhaps harness-bearers).[69]

It may be that, like kern, the Irish galloglass recruits came from a wide range of socio-economic backgrounds. Cowley's 1537 letter to Thomas 'Crumwell' describes galloglass as 'a kynde of sowchynners' (meaning like the Swiss?) who served for wages and not out of love for 'their maister.' Cowley maintains that most ordinary galloglass were 'sklawes' (slaves) recruited from various parts of 'the Irishrie' – by which he presumably meant they were very poor Irishmen given that medieval and Tudor-era Ireland did not have slaves or, it seems, serfs. In a unit of 200 galloglass, says Cowley, only a few would be 'gentlemen' or 'hable men.'[70] There is evidence for high-born Irish galloglass,[71] and the occasional bit of English ancestry, suggesting some of these 'gentlemen' galloglass were, like the 'slaves,' Irishmen.[72]

However, the people really pulling the strings in most galloglass 'battles,' as their units were called, were the members of the great Scots galloglass bloodlines of Mac Domhnaill, Mac Suibhne, Mac Cába (MacCabe), Mac Ruaidhrí (MacRory), Mac Síthigh (MacSheehy) and Mac Dubhghaill (MacDowell). These Scottish families established themselves as considerable local gentry, being both recruiters of galloglass and leaders of communities. A sense of their power becomes clearer through comparison with the English nobility. The Duke of Buckingham had, for instance, 129 men and women on his payroll in 1457.[73] The galloglass chief Toirdhealbhach Caoch Mac Suibhne (died 1399) had, in his 'standing retinue,' 150 men in addition to 'wives and womenfolk,' musicians, poets and lower-status servants.[74]

A study of galloglass landholding also gives a sense of their power. Owen and Terlagh, two brothers of the Mac Síthigh or MacSheehy family of galloglass (neither of whom was the head of the family), held between them something like 3,260 acres in Co. Limerick.[75] The Mac Domhnaill *gallóglaigh* of Tinnakill in Laois, as well as a castle, may have held as much

---

69 W. FitzGerald, 'The MacDonnells of Tinnakill Castle,' *Kildare Archaeological Society Journal*, 4 (1905), p.210.
70 *State Papers, Vol. II: King Henry the Eighth, Part 3* (London: HMSO, 1834), p.448.
71 Cannan, 'If the Father,' p.36.
72 One kern or galloglass (the records were unclear which he was, or perhaps he had been both) had the surname Browne (which may occasionally be a remodelling of a Gaelic name, but in most cases is probably just what it seems: the English surname Brown or Browne). There were also galloglass called Barrett, a surname which arrived with the English invasion, established something of a reputation for themselves – Cannan, *Galloglass*, p.12; Cannan, 'If the Father,' p.36.
73 J. Gillingham, *The Wars of the Roses: Peace & Conflict in 15th Century England* (London: Phoenix Press, 2002), p.32.
74 *Leabhar Chlainne Suibhne*, pp.47–47. One of the illustrations in Derricke's *Image of Irelande* (plate 3) apparently shows, albeit critically and mockingly, this kind of Mac Suibhne entourage, the smartly dressed chief dining outdoors with a woman (perhaps his wife), priest, bard, harper, dog and attendants.
75 Hayes-McCoy, *Scots Mercenary Forces*, p.67.

as 10,000 acres in the sixteenth century.[76] O'Donovan considered Fanad 'lies between Lough Swilly and Mulroy Lough.'[77] If this is correct, the Fanad Mac Suibhne sept had dominance over an area something like 12 kilometres at its widest east to west by the best part of 30 kilometres north to south. The galloglass leadership erected fortified manors such as the Mac Suibhne castles of Rahan (aka McSwyne Castle) and Doe (surely every Gaelic warrior's dream home), and the two Mac Síthigh castles in Co. Limerick of Lisnacullia and Ballyalinan.[78]

MacCabe crest, as recorded in *Fairburn's Crests*.[79] (Artwork by F. Cannan-Braniff)

Other galloglass manors are still to be properly researched, and perhaps even discovered. O'Donovan refers in a letter of 1835 to the castle 'which belonged to a Walter Mac Swyne' at 'Rye' (Irish *raith*: fort) in Tullyaughnish parish, Donegal.[80] Some argue that the ruined castle at Rathmullan – a place O'Donovan called 'the capital of Fanaid[,] MacSweeny Fanaid's country' –[81] is not a Mac Suibhne stronghold, but a castle built in the 1600s after the Mac Suibhne Fanad family had lost possession of the property. Yet we know that there was a Mac Suibhne-founded priory at Rathmullan from

---

76   Cannan, *Galloglass*, p.32.
77   O'Donovan letter of 31st August 1835: RIA 14/C/11/15, p.6.
78   Hayes-McCoy, *Scots Mercenary Forces*, p.36, footnote 1.
79   James Fairburn (revised L. Butters), *Fairburn's Crests* (London: New Orchard Editions, 1989).
80   O'Donovan letter of 1 September 1835: RIA 14/C/11/9, p.10.
81   O'Donovan letter of 30 August 1835: RIA 14/C/11/9, p.2.

the early sixteenth century,[82] and both O'Donovan and Mervyn Archdall, a clergyman-antiquary born in Dublin in 1723, believed there had been a Mac Suibhne castle there as well as a priory (O'Donovan adding that the castle had to be rebuilt by the Mac Suibhne family in 1516 after it fell down).[83] Perhaps in the same period, the Fanad Mac Suibhnes built or at least occupied the little-known Moross Castle in Mulroy Bay (where some stonework survives), and possibly an even less well-known Mac Suibhne castle at Doocarrick (close to Moross, but described in the 1930s as 'all crumbled away').[84]

John Morrill wrote that Tudor and Stuart Ireland had no real 'gentry,' since Ireland and Scotland had a 'baronial' rather than 'gentrified' political culture.[85] But what were these galloglass families, and commanders of kern like the Purcells and Keatings, if not the gentry of their nation? The English of the Tudor period considered gentry, yeomanry and husbandman classes to exist in Ireland – because they did exist. A Philip 'Ketyng' is styled 'gent.' in a document from 1537 recording that he and other 'gentlemen' had fought against 'the King's Irish rebels',[86] and the word 'gent' is used in a document from the Lord Deputy in 1578 addressing the Mac Domhnaill galloglass of Leinster.[87]

While they may have had entourages the same in size as that of an English lord, Ireland's galloglass and kern officer class evidently ranked below Ireland's ducal and magnate class. From what we know, gentry families of galloglass and kern each possessed small numbers (sometimes perhaps only one) of manor houses and castles. The chiefs they served might possess a great deal more stately homes and fortresses – Thomas Butler, 10th Earl of Ormond, who is thought to have been born in 1531, had dozens of castles and manors.[88] Again, the military gentry of Ireland might have estates in the low thousands of acres (Loughmoe, the estate of the head of the Purcells, was, for example, 11,500 acres when it was seized by the Cromwellian government),[89] but the chiefs they served had tens or even hundreds of thousands of acres.[90]

---

82   See my footnote 57, chap. 1.
83   O'Donovan letter of 30 August 1835: RIA 14/C/11/9, p.2; Mervyn Archdall, *Monasticon Hibernicum* (Dublin, 1873), vol. 1, p.213.
84   According to the notes taken about Moross in the late 1930s by school children interviewing locals as part of a folklore projects (published online at Dúchas.ie, Schools' Collection, volume 1089, pp.212 and 309-313).
85   J. Morrill, 'Three Stuart Kingdoms 1603–1689,' in Morrill, *Oxford Illustrated History*, p.76.
86   Hore & Graves, *Social State*, pp.45–46.
87   Borrowes, 'Tennekille Castle,' p.38.
88   Edwards, 'Butler, Thomas', *DIB*.
89   B. Purcell Horan, 'A Brief History of the Purcells of Ireland,' pp.8–9 (available on the website of the Purcell Society), pp.43, 60.
90   Determining the exact size of the really big Irish estates is not easy as they included areas over which claims of overlordship were made, and so on. In the seventeenth century the Ormond estate in Ireland is known to have amounted to nearly 300,000

The wealth of the kern commanders was again markedly less than the lords they followed. In 1546 lands to the value of £10 a year were set aside by the Crown for 'Captain of the King's Kern' William Keating, and in 1588 a Redmond Keating was paid 16d per day by the English administration for his services as captain of 16 kern.[91] This would have been pocket money to an Earl of Kildare, Ormond or Desmond. But no Irish lord would have called the wealth of the leading galloglass families negligible; they had a wealth and social status no kern ever had. In 1578 it was agreed that three Mac Domhnaill galloglass captains serving the Crown in Leinster would receive an annual payment of £300 (apparently to be divided among the three of them).[92] In 1568 the 15th Earl of Desmond had an income just over £1,000 (presumably Irish) from his lands (half of which was disputed).[93] £300 a year was therefore a very substantial sum, showing that although galloglass chiefs were vassals, they were vassals with a formidable social and economic presence.

---

acres: 'Butler, James', *DIB* (entry by M. Perceval-Maxwell). The Earls of Desmond may have ruled over even more (perhaps half a million acres?) before their lands were seized in the 1580s: M. MacCarthy-Morrogh, 'The Munster Plantation, 1583-1641' (Royal Holloway College PhD thesis, 1983), p. 313.

91 Cannan, 'Hags,' p.16.
92 Borrowes, 'Tennekille Castle,' p.38.
93 MacCarthy-Morrogh, 'Munster Plantation,' p.22.

Plate A. Ó Gallchobhair horseman, late 1300s.
(Illustration by Seán Ó Brógain © Helion & Company 2025)
See Colour Plate Commentaries for further information.

Plate B. Galloglass standard bearer in the service of the Butlers of Ormond, early 1400s.
(Illustration by Seán Ó Brógain © Helion & Company 2025)
See Colour Plate Commentaries for further information.

Plate C. 'Rising out' husbandman, mid-1400s.
(Illustration by Seán Ó Brógain © Helion & Company 2025)
See Colour Plate Commentaries for further information.

Plate D. Galloglass fighting for the Earl of Desmond, battle of Piltown, 1462.
(Illustration by Seán Ó Brógain © Helion & Company 2025)
See Colour Plate Commentaries for further information.

Plate E. Kern at the battle of Stoke, 1487.
(Illustration by Seán Ó Brógain © Helion & Company 2025)
See Colour Plate Commentaries for further information.

Plate F. Runner in the Earl of Kildare's service, late 15th century
(Illustration by Seán Ó Brógain © Helion & Company 2025)
See Colour Plate Commentaries for further information.

Plate G. 'Redshank' Highland mercenary in Ireland, c.1500
(Illustration by Seán Ó Brógain © Helion & Company 2025)
See Colour Plate Commentaries for further information.

Plate H. Edmund Purcell, captain of kern, serving with Henry VIII in France, 1544–45.
(Illustration by Seán Ó Brógain © Helion & Company 2025)
See Colour Plate Commentaries for further information.

Plate I. One of Dürer's Irish warriors. (Royal Irish Academy)
See Colour Plate Commentaries for further information.

Plate J. Christ carrying the Cross from the 16th-century 'Book of the De Burgos'.
(The Board of Trinity College Dublin)
See Colour Plate Commentaries for further information.

Plate K. Mid to late 16th century depiction of Irish Men (© Ashmolean Museum, University of Oxford).
See Colour Plate Commentaries for further information.

Plate L. Art Mór Mac Murchadha Caomhánach (© The Board of the British Library).
See Colour Plate Commentaries for further information.

Plate M. Horseman in the 16th-century 'Book of the De Burgos'
(The Board of Trinity College Dublin)
See Colour Plate Commentaries for further information.

Plate N. A member of the Anglo-Irish Preston family, Co. Meath.
(Illustration by Fergus Cannan-Braniff)
See Colour Plate Commentaries for further information.

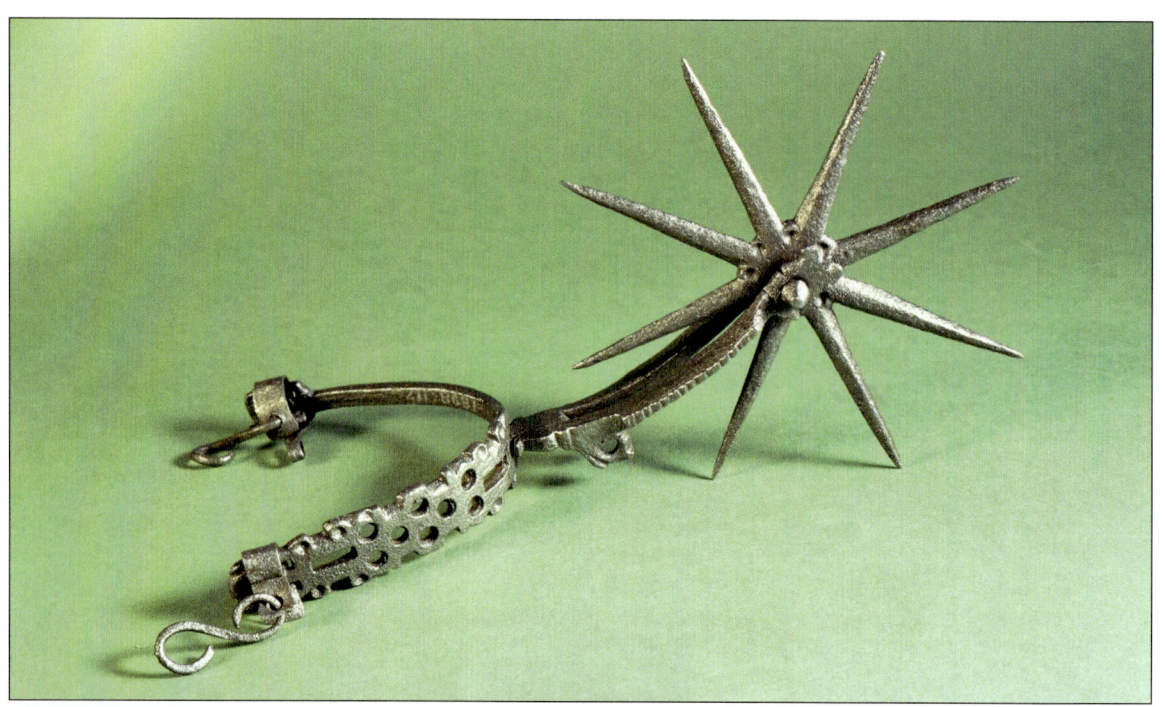

Plate O. Spur found at Clontarf, Co. Dublin.
(© National Museum of Ireland).
See Colour Plate Commentaries for further information.

Plate P. Jacket found as part of a suit of clothes at Kilcommon, Co. Tipperary.
(© National Museum of Ireland)
See Colour Plate Commentaries for further information.

Plate Q. Galloglass at prayer, around 1600, (illustration by Fergus Cannan-Braniff)
See Colour Plate Commentaries for further information.

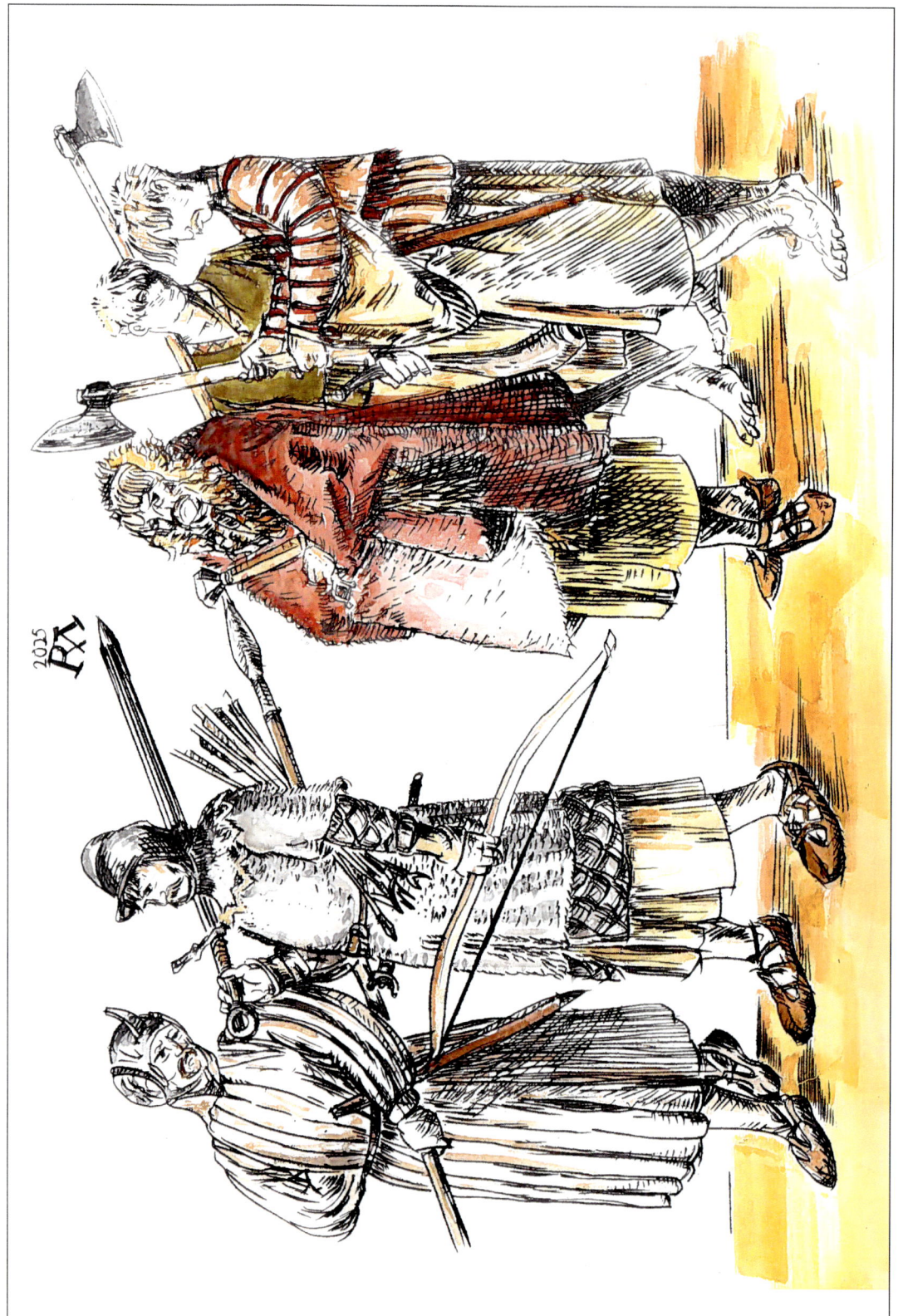

Plate R. A 'corrected' version of Dürer famous depiction of Irish warriors. (Illustration by Russell Moore)
See Colour Plate Commentaries for further information.

3

Body Size & Fitness as a Part of Gaelic Military Selection

They live in thatched cabins and are all big men, handsome and well-built, and fleet as the roe-deer.

> Captain Francisco Cuellar, an Armada survivor, describing the Irish.

…three most handsome sons of fine physique, well built and tall. Had they been a king's sons, they would have looked the part well, I think, and might easily have been knights.

> Fergus of Galloway and his brothers described in Guillaume le Clerc's medieval Arthurian tale.

Although Continental writers – and not just English writers – were often disparaging about Irish and Scottish standards of life, they were routinely impressed by Gaelic bodies. Gaelic dress and ways of life were often condemned by the English, but there was no doubting, as Derricke put it, that the 'Irysh karne' had a 'liuely shape' and, physically, was 'most perfect to behold.'[1] Gaelic soldiers were also tough. St Leger described galloglass and kern in 1543 as 'of suche hardenes, that ther ys no man that ever I sawe, that will or can endure the paynes and evill fare that they will sustayne.'[2] Repackaging old accounts like Gerald of Wales and Gildas, William Caxton's 1480 *Description of Britain* took the view that Scottish people were 'very beautifully formed' but made 'repellent' by their ugly clothing.[3]

---

1   Derricke, *Image of Irelande*, plate 1.
2   Lydon, 'Scottish Soldier Abroad,' in Duffy, *Robert the Bruce's Irish Wars*, p.106.
3   William Caxton (M. Collins, ed.), *The Description of Britain* (London: Guild,

What, then, could be more fundamental to the writing of Gaelic military history than the question of what the warriors actually looked like? Fitness and strength training were clearly a major part of traditional Gaelic warriorhood, but historians attribute the health and toughness of Gaelic soldiers to natural or chance factors, rather than to the lifestyle choices the Irish and Scots made, and the effort that their commanders went to in selecting the fittest and strongest members of their communities to be their soldiers.

Height

It was reported in the reign of Henry VIII, that 3,000 'very tall men' dressed 'for the most part' in mail shirts and armed with 'long swords and long bows,' and a few guns, were transported in galleys from the Highlands to Ireland by 'tall maryners.'[4] There is nothing ridiculous in considering the possibility that Ireland and Scotland had a decent supply of tall, fit recruits. It might be possible given that Gaelic armies were recruited entirely from the countryside, meaning, one would think, less disease, a more outdoor way of life, and perhaps a better diet. Many of the women must have been physically formidable too if the sixteenth century depiction of a strong-looking Irishwoman by de Heere is to be believed; she is absolutely the ugly-in-dress/beautiful-in-body Gael mentioned in Caxton's *Description*.

Likewise, a poem which Katharine Simms believes might date from the 1340s–1380s,[5] celebrates a force of 'Tall men' led by 'John M'Sween' sailing luxury galleys to take back their old Scottish fortress, Castle Sween.[6] Historians will likely dismiss this talk of tall men as poetic flourishes, while a few will credulously believe every word of it. Yet the Scotsman Adam Loutfut, Kintyre Pursuivant, made an 'ynglis' reworking of parts of Vegetius' *De Re Militari* in 1494, and is clear that good soldiers must have 'courage and hardynes' and 'manheid & strength of body,' and that some occupations including 'barbours, writaris & talyeouris' are unlikely to become useful soldiers since what use is a 'needle or razor or pen against a spear or axe'?[7] In other words, it is possible that words like 'tall' are describing *actual military selection systems*, where the most physically impressive men were targeted for recruitment – and not just galloglass but also redshanks and quite possibly kern as well. Irish chiefs, Scots lairds and English peers all looked for the same kind of man for their retinues – a tall, well-presented man,

---

1988), p.145.

4   Quoted in D. Gregory, *History of the Western Highlands and Isles of Scotland from AD 1493 to AD 1625 with a Brief Introductory Sketch From AD 80 to AD 1493* (Vancouver: Eremitical Press, 2009), p.127.

5   Simms, 'Images of the Galloglass, in Duffy, *World of the Galloglass*, p.111.

6   T. M'Laughlan (trans. and ed.) *The Dean of Lismore's Book* (Edinburgh: Edmonston & Douglas, 1862), p.151.

7   Quoted in Allmand, *The De Re Militari*, p.235.

BODY SIZE & FITNESS AS A PART OF GAELIC MILITARY SELECTION

ideally from a respectable family, who could appear as the embodiment of their lord's splendour and power, but who would also stay in line and know his place. Born in London in 1524 or 1525, the antiquary John Stow records the retinue of 'tall and comely gentlemen and yeoman' kept by the Duke of Somerset, and the Earl of Oxford's 'one hundred tall yeomen' in livery.[8]

The same philosophy was followed by the Irish when it came to selecting their warhorses. Philip O'Sullivan Beare, a writer and poet born in Co. Cork in the 1590s, recounts that warhorses were selected for their size and 'strength, courage and ferocity,'[9] and Stanihurst claims Irish horsemen would only ride stallions (which sounds like a wild boast, rather than the truth).[10]

Art Mór Mac Murchadha, a dogged opponent of Richard II in Ireland, was described by Creton (who had seen him) as 'a fine large man, wondrously active' as well as 'stern.'[11] Art's size may explain his Gaelic alias of *Mór* ('big,' 'large,' 'great').[12] Thomas Fitzgerald, the 10th Earl of Kildare (known as 'Silken Thomas', and executed by Henry VIII in 1537), was remembered as tall and handsome, though his half-brother, the 11th Earl, was considered small.[13] The problem, of course, is establishing what is meant by words like 'tall' and 'big.' The 'big' Irish people Cuellar saw may only have been big in relation to the people of his own nation, and may not have been particularly big or tall by modern standards (or at all big and tall by modern standards). But it is an error to imagine that everyone was tiny in the past. Edward I of England is reckoned to have been about 6ft 2in, Edward IV was about 6ft 4in and Henry VIII was over 6ft. An iron barbute-style helmet of *c.* 1400 was found in or around 1835 in the loam of a crannog on Lough Henney (Co. Down), where some mail and the remains of a very tall man – supposedly around eight foot tall! – were also discovered.[14]

All the same, it is a fact that most premodern Europeans were shorter and slighter than they are today, making a unit of tall men, such as that raised by Alexander MacDonnell, 3rd Earl of Antrim, for

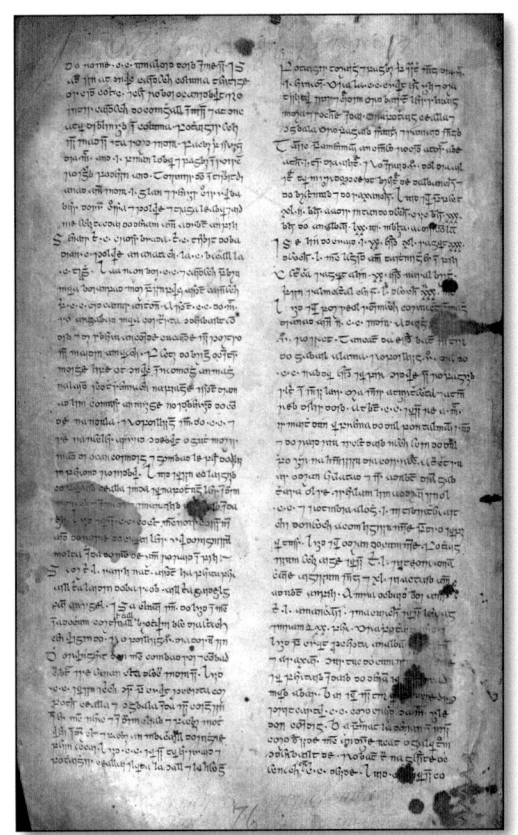

Page of bardic verse celebrating Donal Mac Suibhne, lord of Fanad from 1570. The poem says Donal selected the fiercest and strongest individuals to be his soldiers. (Reproduced by kind permission of the Royal Irish Academy©)

---

8   Stow, *Survey of London*, p.115.
9   Quoted in McGettigan, *Richard II*, p.81.
10 Stanihurst, *Great Deeds*, p.123.
11 Quoted in McGettigan, *Richard II*, p.176.
12 'MacMurrough Kavanagh,' *DIB* (entry by E. O'Byrne).
13 'Fitzgerald, Thomas,' *ODNB* (entry by S. G. Ellis); 'Fitzgerald, Gerald,' *ODNB* (entry by D. Finnegan).
14 C. Bourke, 'A Medieval Helmet from Lough Henney, Co. Down,' *Lecale Miscellany*, no. 8 (1990), pp.5–7.

the war against William of Orange, all the more impressive. Rather than innovating, it may well be that MacDonnell was following the traditional Highland/Irish system of recruitment.[15] The Rev. John Mackenzie served as a Williamite chaplain during the siege of Derry, and reckoned that the 1,200 men recruited by MacDonnell from Ulster and the Highlands were 'all near six feet high.'[16] Bear in mind the average height of an Englishman during the 1600s was probably about 5ft 6in or 5ft 7in[17] (and one can hazard it was about the same for Scotsmen and Irishmen), and you realise that a unit of men around six feet would have looked dauntingly large – not just in the 1600s or in medieval Ireland but at any point in history, anywhere in the world, before the second half of the twentieth century. It was mentioned as a matter of Gaelic pride in the 1840s by James Logan, a writer on tartan and clans, that when the Earl of Sutherland raised a unit of 1,100 Highlanders in 1759, 300 of the recruits were 'upwards of five feet eleven inches in height,' and that because 'the men were so tall,' Sutherland's officers formed no 'light company.'[18]

Galloglass & Size

Given tall people were comparatively rare, it is striking that three Tudor accounts – one from Dymmok and two from Stanihurst – state as fact that size was an important characteristic of the galloglass. Dymmok, apparently writing at the end of the 1500s, tells us that 'Gallogass ar pycked and scelected men of great and mightie bodies, crewell without compassion.'[19] Stanihurst says in his contributions to Holinshed's *Chronicles* (written in the 1570s, based on his studies with Edmund Campion) that 'galloglasse' are 'tall of stature, big of lime, burly of body, wel and strongly timberd.'[20]

---

15   That such a custom could still exist among the MacDonnells in the late 1600s is perfectly feasible. Alexander spent much of his childhood in England, but his older brother Randall (the 2nd Earl) was 'bred the highland way,' wearing 'neither hat, cap, nor shoe, nor stocking' until he was seven or eight: *DIB*, 'MacDonnell, Randall' (entry by J. Ohlmeyer). T. Clavin adds that Alexander and Randall's father (1st Earl) 'raised his children in the highland fashion' and 'maintained a traditional Gaelic retinue.' – *DIB*, 'MacDonnell, Sir Randal mac Sorley'; also *DIB*, 'MacDonnell, Alexander' (entry by M. Ó Siochrú).
16   John Mackenzie, *Memorials of the Siege of Derry*, ed. W. D. Killen (Belfast, 1861), p.7. Some said the deploying of this regiment to Derry was delayed by the Earl or his officers trying to ensure that their soldiers were of this height.
17   'Highs and Lows of an Englishman's Average Height Over 2000 Years' (website of Oxford University, 2017); G. Galofré-Vilà, A. Hinde & A. M. Guntupalli, 'Heights Across the Last 2,000 Years in England,' *Research in Economic History*, 34 (2018), pp.67–98; Mortimer, *Time Traveller's Guide to Medieval England*, p.36.
18   James Logan & R. R. McIan, *The Clans of the Scottish Highlands* (London: Chancellor Press, 1985), p.70.
19   Dymmok, *Treatice*, p.7.
20   Stanihurst, *Irish Chronicle*, p.114.

Then in his 1594 *De Rebus in Hibernia Gestis* (*Great Deeds in Ireland*) Stanihurst wrote that galloglass are 'men of great stature, muscled beyond what is normal.'[21] Perhaps there was something in the genes as well as diet and training: O'Donovan recalled coming across 'two sons of McSweeney' in a cabin in Gweedore, Donegal, in 1835, '…with thighs as thick as two fat bullocks, playing with deafening sound, the one upon bagpipes, the other upon the fiddle.'[22]

The galloglass' fatty, but also organic and unprocessed diet (beef, beef and more beef, with helpings of pork, butter and milk are what the records mention) no doubt helped build their size.[23] Historians should be aware, though, that in medieval and early modern English the word 'meat' sometimes simply meant food; so the classic galloglass diet may not have been quite such a non-stop carnivorous protein fest.[24] But, given that animal flesh and feasting were key currencies of homage and fealty in Gaelic Ireland and Scotland, there must have been a lot of feasting while the peasantry scratched a living outside. If the galloglass' food was as plentiful as the

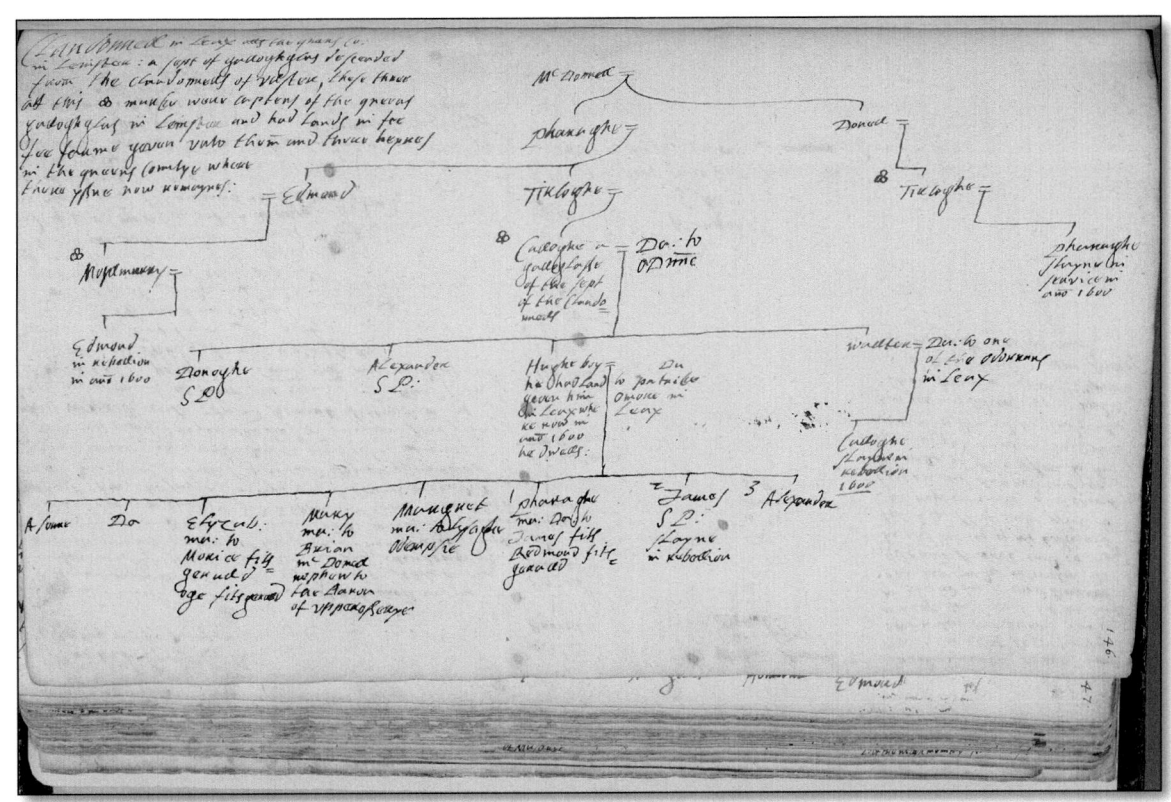

Family tree made at the start of the seventeenth century of the Mac Domhnaill or MacDonnell galloglass of Leinster, who for a time served the English administration in Ireland. Aodh Buidhe appears on the tree as 'Hughe boy' along with one relative described as 'slayne in service', another as 'in rebellion' and two as 'slayne in rebellion'. (© Lambeth Palace Library, Carew Ms 635 f.146r)

---

21 Stanihurst, *Great Deeds*, p.123.
22 Quoted in 'Mac Suibhne (McSweeney), Tarlach,' *DIB* (entry by D. McCabe).
23 Cannan, *Galloglass*, pp.27–28.
24 For instance, Sir Anthony Fitzherbet, Justice of the Common Pleas in Henry VIII's reign, reminded servants not to forget to 'gyve thy horse meate.' – Quoted in J. Pullein-Thompson, *Horses and Their Owners* (London: Nelson, 1970), p.40. See also *OED*, 'meat.'

records imply it must have made them quite hefty, especially as they grew older – perhaps in the way that Henry VIII morphed from an athletic man weighing about 15 stone in his twenties into an invalid with a 'sorre legge' weighing perhaps 28 stone by the time of his death.[25] Possibly something similar happened to the galloglass captain Aodh Buidhe (anglicised to 'Hugh Boy', Yellow Hugh) Mac Domhnaill of Tinnakill, of whom George Carew wrote in 1600: '…in the Queen's County there is a Galloglass of good livelihood called Hugh Boy M'Calloghe. His sons, as I understand, are in rebellion, but himself is an aged corpulent man, and lives in neutrality.'[26]

Maybe one of the dangers of being a full-time galloglass was that it could make you overweight! More's *Utopia* alleges that full-time military retainers (their nationality is not stated) were prone to lose their 'powerful physiques' becoming 'soft and flabby by sitting around doing nothing.'[27]

In bad times, though, the galloglass profession could inflict the reverse on a man's body, the galloglass leader Ustian Mac Domhnaill, who fought hard against English encroachment in the 1570s and 1580s, being described by a modern historian as 'gaunt and half-starved' when he threw in the towel and sought terms.[28] Besides, some of the galloglass' opponents were substantial men too: the Anglo-Irish nobleman Sir William Darcy was known as 'Great Darsey' because of his physical appearance, and he experienced being knocked to his knees by Clanrickard's Mac Suibhne captain of galloglass, who challenged Darcy at the Battle of Knockdoe.[29]

This is where regular training and physical exercise came in to avoid your galloglass and kern becoming restless and unruly or simply a gang of out of shape Falstaffs. If a galloglass was a full-time retained warrior in the house of a chief he would have had the time to develop an impressively strong, supple body through exercise and weapons training, so long as his commander was sensible enough to keep his men fit and ready. There is nothing modern about toned bodies – think of the thickly-muscled figures Michelangelo depicts in the Sistine Chapel (though he appears to have made their heads artificially small so as to increase the size of the body),[30] or the toned people Dürer drew, engraved and painted.[31] The Irishmen in

---

25 C.R. Chalmers & E. J. Chaloner, '500 Years Later: Henry VIII, Leg Ulcers and the Course of History,' *Journal of the Royal Society of Medicine* (2009), pp.512–517.
26 Quoted in FitzGerald, 'MacDonnells of Tinnakill Castle,' p.212.
27 More, *Utopia*, p.24.
28 'MacDonnell, Ustian,' *DIB* (entry by A. McCormack & T. Clavin).
29 'Darcy, Sir William,' *DIB* (entry by S. G. Ellis); Hayes-McCoy, *Irish Battles*, p.63. The galloglass captain was then promptly assailed by a Palesman, Nangle of Navan, Hayes-McCoy, *op. cit.*
30 Michelangelo's preparatory drawings in the British Museum show these details of physique particularly vividly.
31 See especially Dürer's depiction (which in a humanist renaissance spirit seems to celebrate rather than condemn human physical potential) of Adam in his 1504 engraving of Adam and Eve; also Dürer's brush and ink nude self-portrait of *c*. 1505 in the Staatliche Kunstsammlung, Weimar; and his muscular figure of Christ in the oil panels of the Crucifixion and the Nailing to the Cross included in the

the Ashmolean 'AFTER THE QVICKE' woodcut have extremely impressive calf and arm muscles, and big hands. The sleeve of the man on the picture's far left is pushed back, revealing a very powerful-looking arm. Admittedly, the six men have hair that could do with a brush, but they look fit and athletic. Their limbs look long, and they look just like the 'tall men' the accounts describe.

In the words of a survey commissioned in 1597 of the 26th MacCarthy Mór's domains, 'Kearnty' were 'a companye of light footmen,' and yet, unlike many later light infantry units, it may be that kern were also often selected from the biggest available men.[32] The rather lolloping gait of the Irish kern in the Cowdray engraving gives the impression that they are tall men. When Irish forces were modernised at the end of the 1500s, it was the galloglass who were reequipped as pikemen and the kern who became musketeers. This implies that kern were the smaller men, since contemporary military theory recommended that pikemen should be big men.[33] Yet historians miss the point when they conclude the changing of kern into musketeers was all about body size or pure military rationality, because questions of prestige and class doubtless influenced these military decisions. The pike was regarded in England, and elsewhere in Europe, as more genteel than the musket.[34] Perhaps, then, the decision to convert galloglass into pike and kern into shot was more driven by the reformers' desire to not offend the galloglass' traditional precedence over kern than about anyone's body size.

'Togha' Warriors – Selected Men

That being so, it is all too easy to focus exclusively on the physical elements of these accounts and overlook the other important characteristics which are described. The 'grim' manner, and the body confidence that exercise

---

    Seven Sorrows of the Virgin (c. 1496–1497 in the collection of the Gemäldegalrie Alte Meister, Dresden.

32 'The Desmond Survey,' published online at CELT.

33 The experienced Scottish professional soldier Sir James Turner (born 1615) recommended a separating of taller and shorter recruits, urging that 'the tallest, biggest and strongest should be order'd to carry Pikes …. I have known Muskets given to those of the biggest stature, and Pikes to the unworthiest and silliest of the Company' – quoted in P. Haythornthwaite, *The English Civil War 1642–1651: An Illustrated Military History* (Poole: Blandford Press, 1983), p.44.

34 Richard Elton, *Compleat Body of the Art Military* (1650) asserted the pike was more honourable than the musket on the basis that it had existed 'before there was any knowledge of the Musket' – quoted in Keith Roberts, *Soldiers of the English Civil War (1): Infantry* (Oxford: Osprey, 1989), p.22. As Captain Thomas Venn put it in a book on the art of war published in 1672, 'the Gentlemen of the Pike craveth the precedence' (quoted *ibid.*, p.2). Barry, being an old hand in the Spanish service, states in *Discourse of Military Discipline* (Brussels: Widdow of John Mommart, 1634), p.9, that 'the pike and corselett [body armour] a mongste foote men is of moste estimation.'

and training give, may have made Gaelic soldiers seem bigger than they really were, as would the thick padded armour often worn by redshanks and galloglass. Vegetius, at any rate, points out that the 'height of a man' is secondary to his strength of body and character, and validating that observation is a story about a contest of Highland athletes held at Dunvegan, apparently in the 1500s, which was won by an absolute underdog, a small but very strong man named Pól Crubach (Paul the Limping/Lame/Disabled).[35]

Indeed, it is not galloglass body size that Gaelic poetry stresses but the pluck, loyalty, military skill and liberality of their officers, and what Simms has termed the Gaelic nobility's 'Spartan' cult of toughness.[36] Something approaching a reference to galloglass physique is, though, contained in verse 29 of a poem which was composed in honour of Donal Mac Suibhne, ruler of Fanad from 1570, and which is now in the collection of the Royal Irish Academy. The poem says Donal chose only the strongest men of Fanad to be his warriors: 'D'feraib Fanad .... loich 'ga togha ar tresi a lámh...'[37]

The key words here are: 'loich' (modern Irish *laoich*, 'warrior,' possibly a mighty, fierce, conquering or young warrior); 'togha' (modern Irish *togha* = 'choicest' or 'picked'); and 'tresi' (modern Irish *treis*, 'strong'). We should acknowledge that the poem is not necessarily describing galloglass, given that galloglass chiefs appear to have commanded a wider range of soldiers than just *gallóglaigh*.[38] Nor does the Royal Irish Academy poem specify whether the selection of 'strong' men refers to something specific like lifting power or a more general athleticism; most likely it is the poet's attempt at conveying the kind of all-round physical power and commitment that characterised your model galloglass. Being big and strong seems to have been a route to a social advancement in the Gaeltacht if you could get yourself taken on by a constable, in the sense that galloglass, redshanks and kern had access to free cuisine and hospitality, and they had an unpleasant power over the civilian population.

Not that it was always easy to get the kind of men constables wanted. There was no national army or national selection standards and so, if they

---

35 A. Nicolson (A. Maclean ed.), *History of Skye* (Portree: Maclean Press, 1930, revised edition), p.61.
36 Simms, 'Images of the Galloglass, in Duffy, *World of the Galloglass*, p.119.
37 RIA MS 475 (24/P/25), f. 76v. As my starting point I am using here Katharine Simms' transcription and discussion of this passage in 'Images of the Galloglass,' in Duffy, *World of the Galloglass*, p.118.
38 For example, in 1588 the Government hired kern led by a Mac Síthigh: Hayes-McCoy, 'Gallóglach Axe,' p.104n. Likewise, Viscount de Perellós, who died around 1419, recounted meeting 'King O'Neill's constable with a hundred men on horseback,' and it possible this constable was the galloglass leader Eoin Maol Mac Domhnaill: McGettigan, *Richard II*, p.87. Also, a list included at the end of Dymmok's *Treatice*, p.29 of forces 'imployed in the rebellion, 28 April 1599' states that 'the Mac Swynes cuntry' has 500 'foote' and 30 horse.

had land, commanders would have trawled the area for the best fighters, inspiring, cajoling or bullying those they found to join up.[39]

If an itinerant mercenary galloglass company, a captain would have to assemble a unit out of whatever drifters, outlaws and ex-soldiers came their way. Cowley must have seen or heard about a very rag-tag galloglass because his letter to Thomas Cromwell asserts the rank-and-file 'slaves' were disunited and ready to swap sides without a second thought.[40]

No doubt Gaelic units varied in quality; but that is a feature of all armies throughout history. It is nevertheless noteworthy that the Royal Irish Academy Mac Suibne poem's inclusion of the word *togha* chimes with Dymmok's reference to galloglass being 'pycked and scelected men.' Could Dymmok, who writes like someone with a good knowledge of military matters, have meant something more systematic than simply picking out the biggest of the local rural lads you came across, perhaps a selection system resembling that which Dymmok was familiar with in his own country? There is no reason to believe that, if there was a sufficient pool of recruits (and there often seems to have been in Scotland), galloglass officers were incapable of devising actual tests – perhaps something resembling the English 'Yeomen of the Crown,' who in the 1400s were to be selected from the 'most semely persons, clenely and the strongest archers,' who were to be 'chosen and tryed out of every lordes house in Ynglond.'[41] While one is wary of reading too much into Dymmok's use of the word selected, it is important to consider what Jim Bradbury wrote in his study of medieval archers:

> The term 'selected' men has generally been ignored as having no real significance …. When recruitment procedures emerge from the gloom of obscurity in the later medieval period, it can be seen that the general practice was not to call upon every available man, but to review those liable, and 'select' the best.[42]

In addition to physique, recurring themes in European medieval selection were:

1. class status
2. who owed military service as part of tenancy agreements
3. who had the appropriate equipment

---

39 Perhaps in the manner of the Duke of Athole, who in the 1700s allegedly rounded up his 'volunteer' Highland soldiers with blood hounds: Palmer, *Rambling Soldier*, p.10.
40 *State Papers, Vol. II: King Henry the Eighth, Part 3*, p.448.
41 Quoted in C. Bartlett, *English Longbowman 1330–1515* (Oxford: Osprey, 2020), p.7.
42 J. Bradbury, *The Medieval Archer* (Woodbridge: Boydell Press, 1997), p.172.

We can probably add a fourth consideration (which will resonate with anyone with experience of organising re-enactment groups): who could be depended upon to actually turn up on the day. When the system worked, it meant you were fielding your community's best. Scotland seems to have been pretty efficient at finding quality recruits. Writing in the 1500s, Robert Lindsay of Pitscottie recounted that a MacLean, who was 'ane gret man of the Yleis of Scotland' raised for James IV 'ane companie' of 600 'schoisin men' with bows, hand-and-a-half swords and mail shirts.[43]

Physical Training

Athleticism, and who exhibited a controlled aggression, might have been a means of selection. If an old tale concerning Tormad, 12th Chief of the MacLeods, is to be believed, traditional Highland sports – rock throwing, swimming, wrestling, jumping, running, archery – were used in a modern way as military selection tests. The story goes that, in the 1500s, Tormad was so fearful of assassination that he formed, in the words of the Gaelic scholar Alexander Nicolson (born on Skye in 1884), 'a bodyguard of twelve picked men.' To qualify as one of Tormad's bodyguards, continues Nicolson, clansmen had to 'excel in leaping, wrestling, throwing the stone and in caber-tossing'; for those who passed this test, there was the final challenge of having to 'wrench off with one hand a bull's leg at the knee. If they succeeded in this, they were admitted to the chief's circle, the '*Buannachan*' or 'Bullies'.[44] How interesting that Nicolson opted for bully rather than 'billeted soldier' and the more strictly accurate but also more sanitised translation of *buanna* preferred by modern academics![45]

The trials Tormad's prospective guards undertook are essentially the fitness regime of the medieval European knight (and indeed Asian warriors). A comparable line-up of activities designed to develop supple, strong and tough bodies – rock throwing (also a Highland sport),[46] wrestling, javelin throwing, sword and buckler fighting, acrobatics and quarter-staff combat – is shown in a fifteenth century picture of young men training in

---

43 Robert Lindsay of Pitscottie (Æ. J. G Mackay, ed.), *The Historie and Cronicles of Scotland* (Edinburgh: Scottish Text Society, 1899), volume 1, p.274.

44 Nicolson, *History of Skye*, pp.43–44.

45 Nicolson, *History of Skye*, p.61. Even better is Malcolm MacLennan's definition of *buanna* in *Pronouncing and Etymological Dictionary* (Stonoway & Aberdeen: Acair & Aberdeen University Press, 1982): 'a billeted soldier ... a mercenary developed to a parasite.'

46 Touring the Scottish Highlands in 1769, Thomas Pennant found that many of the 'ancient' (his word) sports, 'such as archery, hunting, fowling and fishing, are now disused,' but that 'throwing the putting-stone, or stone of strength, as they call it' was still practised. Thomas Pennant, *A Tour in Scotland 1769* (Edinburgh: Birlinn, 2019), p.128.

Modena's Biblioteca Estense.[47] Vegetius was clear that exercise, swimming, leaping, route marches and weapons-drill will make a good soldier.[48] The difference is that Gaelic Ireland and Scotland were still following these traditional training methods aimed at developing supreme individual skills after most of western Europe had moved on to the unit drilling of the 'military revolution.' Martin Martin, a man born and bred to Gaelic traditions (his father was chamberlain of Trotternish on the Isle of Skye and served in Montrose's Royalist army), uses the same word as the Royal Irish Academy Mac Suibhne poem when he writes of Hebridean chiefs in days gone by having had a '*guard de corps*' of '*lucht-taeh*' ('household people,' i.e. household soldiers).[49]

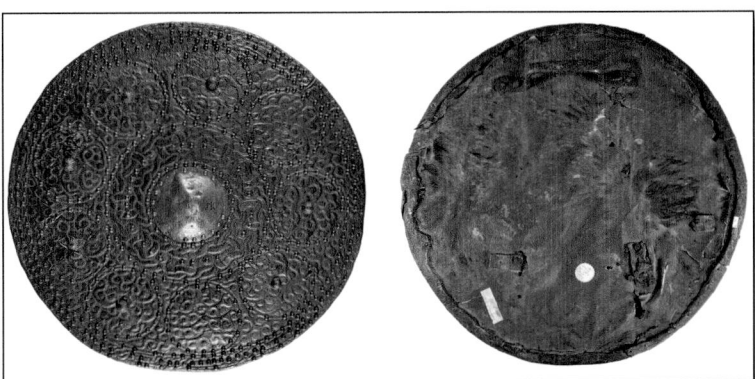 

The earliest dated targe, made for the Highland Nobleman Sir Donald MacKay of Strathnaver, the boss bears the date 1623. Targes were used by medieval Scottish soldiers, and the round, wooden, leather-covered shields used by both Irish and Scots were probably not fundamentally different to this example. (Hunterian Museum, University of Glasgow)

The term *lucht-tighe* was also used in Ireland where in the twelfth and thirteenth centuries it appears to have meant the household warriors of a chief. In the fifteenth and sixteenth century the term appears to have morphed to mean the so-called 'mensal' lands set aside for the chief. This possibly reflects a centralising of power by chiefs, as they attempted to move from the old ideas of a clan being an assembly of people, in favour of notions that a clan was principally about themselves, their command over professional units of soldiers, their control of land, and their granting of land to galloglass and other household officials.[50]

---

47 Count Baldassare Castiglione's *Book of the Courtier* (written 1508-1516) furthermore recommended the noble classes practice running, jumping, wrestling and weight-throwing.
48 Vegetius, *De Re Militari*, p.20 onwards.
49 Martin Martin, *A Description of the Western Isles of Scotland* (Edinburgh: Birlinn, 2018), p.78.
50 Simms, *Kings to Warlords*, p.176.

Chiefs, clans and hereditary professionals survived longer in Scotland than in Ireland. In Ireland that world died out in the 1600s; in Scotland it endured until Culloden and the clearances. Indeed, although Martin lived long after the Middle Ages – he died, perhaps in his late fifties, 'of an Asthma' in 1718 – he writes of galloglass and household warriors as customs that were by no means ancient history: 'Every chieftain had a bold armour-bearer, whose business was always to attend the person of his master night and day to prevent any surprise, and this man was called *galloglach*.'[51]

Martin tells us it was customary for the galloglass to receive 'a double portion of meat … The measure of meat usually given him is called to this day *bieyfir*, that is, a man's portion, meaning thereby an extraordinary man, whose strength and courage distinguished him from the common sort.'[52] The role of armour-bearer was something Highlanders still cared about in the days of Bonnie Prince Charlie, an eyewitness account from Alexander Carlyle recording that among the Jacobite army in 1745 was a 'Fine Brisk little [*note he was not a big man!*] well Dress'd Highlander arm'd Cap a Pie with Pistols and Dirk and Broadsword,' who had 'that Morning been Armour Bearer to the Duke of Perth.'[53]

Wrestling

Re-enactment does not, for safety reasons, feature much grappling, grabbing, kicking or taking hold of your opponent's weapon, but real medieval battles would have involved a lot of that. Vegetius did not mention wrestling, but it may be that by the late Middle Ages it was regarded as a useful skill for soldiers. A fifteenth century French or Italian copy of *De Re Militari* features an illustration of soldiers wrestling,[54] and a recommendation that soldiers wrestle was likewise added to a German-language copy of *De Re Militari* made in or around 1438.[55] Again, Talhoffer's 'Fight Book' devotes 32 illustrations to wrestling, emphasising that being able to disarm and shut down their opponent is as important, or even more so, as being able to fight with weapons.[56]

Wrestling is a traditional Highland sport. A grave-slab from Fan an Charta, today at St Mary's Church, Killybegs, is said to commemorate a Mac Suibhne Tír Boghaine of Rahan castle. While the slab's dominant decoration is an axe-armed figure on the top left of the panel resembling a

---

51 Martin, *Description*, p.79.
52 Martin, *Description*, p.79.
53 Alexander Carlyle, *Anecdotes and Characters of the Times*, ed. J. Kinsley (London: Oxford University Press, 1973), pp.75–76.
54 New York Morgan Library Ms M.634, f.3r; see Allmand, *The De Re Militari*, p.199.
55 The text is Seitenstetten Stiftsbibliothek 65, ff. 2-146v; for the analysis, again see Allmand, *The De Re Militari*, pp.193–194.
56 Talhoffer, *Medieval Combat*, p.17 and plates 190–221.

galloglass, at the bottom left of the slab are two figures who, assuming they are not hugging, seem to be grappling or wrestling.

As well as keeping a man physically and mentally fit, wrestling requires no expensive equipment. Moreover, the soldier who knows unarmed combat has a huge advantage over the soldier who only knows how to use weapons, as unarmed combat (as do contact sports) keeps soldiers fit, gives them physical confidence, and makes them creative and inventive in combat. These observations may have been especially true during the late Middle Ages when armies were growing larger, and there perhaps began to be more emphasis on fighting in formation, meaning the space around the individual fighter may have become more confined. The skill level of the soldiers may have been higher too as leaders began to rely more on mercenaries and contracted professionals. If we are right that late medieval battles had become densely packed places involving highly skilled combatants, one can imagine that the opportunities for swinging a large weapon like a galloglass axe were reduced, as great blocks of human beings pressed against one another, making the fighting very close and personal, and offering fewer chances to pull away from opponents and find a less packed part of the battlefield to fight in. Double-handed weaponry could be used in the initial advance and clash; but if the advance stalled, one needed to know how to be creative with fighting methods.

Holding wrestling matches would furthermore have been a useful way of keeping one's soldiers busy, focusing potentially rebellious energies into a disciplined, relatively safe activity. After all, if you employ a full-time force of warriors, you are, warned Thomas More, keeping 'savage pets.'[57] We do not know whether Gaelic wrestling had a particular style, or whether there were regional, family or clan styles, but it was clearly followed seriously as a sport with rules. An international contest took place when the Highlander Rorie Mackenzie, who was imprisoned on Bass Rock by James IV of Scotland, beat a visiting Italian champion in a wrestling match – as a reward King James set Mackenzie free.[58]

Wrestling could also be used judicially as a form of duel. In the fifteenth century, Ruaidhrí Mac Suibhne settled a succession dispute with his uncle Donnchadh Garbh in a wrestling match. Ruaidhrí won,[59] and such events demonstrate the high level of physical training undertaken by the professional soldiers of the old Gaelic nations, and not a reliance on mere adrenalin and brute force.

---

57 More, *Utopia*, p.24.
58 R. MacGregor, *Memorials of the Bass Rock* (Edinburgh: James Gremmell, 1881), pp.23–24.
59 'Mac Suibhne Fánad,' in Gillespie, 'Gaelic Families of Donegal,' in Nolan, Ronayne & Dunlevy, *Donegal*.

Health & Age

Despite the wrestling, rock throwing and other fitness activities, we cannot ignore the fact that we are discussing an age when ordinary life was often cut short by disease, accident and casual violence. Rural Ireland and Scotland may have been relatively healthy places, but we must not exaggerate the physical condition of Gaelic soldiers.[60] Even those deemed fit for military service would have had scars, old injuries and missing teeth. The 9th Earl of Ormond was called *bacach* (lame) from a leg wound received in France in 1513 as a teenage soldier in Henry VIII's army.[61] 'Bacach' became, as well, the nickname of Muircheartach Ó Conchobhair or O'Connor, who defeated the O'Donnells at Assaroe in 1388, and Conn Ó Néill, who was created Earl of Tyrone in 1542.[62] *Carrach* (scabby/scaly/mangy) suggests unpleasant skin conditions, and this was the nickname of a number of noblemen including the galloglass leader Eoin Mac Domhnaill (killed in 1466) and Art Mór Mac Murchadha's brother Tomás (who drowned in 1402).[63] The vulnerability of the human eye to accident, infection and violence is demonstrated by the soubriquet *caoch* (one-eyed) given to at least two galloglass, Toirdhealbhach Mac Suibhne of Fanad, and Conor Mac Domhnaill (whose son died in battle in 1526).[64]

There was, as well, a range of ages among the recruits. Although traditional Irish law had stated adulthood started at 17 years old,[65] 16 to 60 was a fairly standard age range for military service in medieval and renaissance Ireland as well as in England and Scotland.[66] There was, however, nothing to stop an officer accepting a younger boy or older man into a unit. The 10th Earl of Ormond can only have been about 16 when he took part in the Battle of Pinkie against Scotland in 1547.[67] Born 1456/7, the 8th Earl of Kildare was commander of 24 'spearmen' (probably meaning spear/lance-armed horsemen) when he was about 15 or 16.[68] Despite disease, war and

---

60 Skeletons, ranging in date from the seventh to early seventeenth century, that were unearthed at Ballyhanna in Donegal exhibited many signs of hard physical activity and disease – probably more so than injury through violence. See C. J. McKenzie, & E. M. Murphy, *Life and Death in Medieval Gaelic Ireland: The Skeletons from Ballyhanna, Co. Donegal* (Dublin: Four Courts Press, 2018).
61 Edwards, 'Butler [Bocach], James,' *ODNB*.
62 'O'Connor (Ó Conchobhair), Domhnall,' *DIB* (entry by E. O'Byrne); 'O'Neill, Conn Bacach, first earl of Tyrone,' *ODNB* (entry by C. Maginn).
63 Family tree in FitzGerald, 'MacDonnells of Tinnakill'; McGettigan, *Richard II*, pp.97, 102.
64 E. D. Borrowes, 'Tennekille Castle, Portarlington, and Glimpses of the MacDonnells,' *Ulster Journal of Archaeology*, 1st series, vol. 2 (1854), p.36; Cannan, *Galloglass*, p.19. Unless, of course, the early writers meant *charrach* (crazy)?
65 E. MacNeill's introduction to Hayes-McCoy, *Scots Mercenary Forces*, p.viii.
66 'Army,' *OCIH*; Bartlett, *English Longbowman*, p.5; Cannan, *Galloglass*, p.14.
67 'Butler, Thomas' *ODNB* (entry by. D. Edwards).
68 'FitzGerald, Gerald (Gearóid Mór)', *DIB* (entry by M. A. Lyons).

violence, life expectancy was not quite as poor in medieval Europe as is often claimed – if, and this is a major *if*, you could survive childhood. In 1521, the same year that he drew his Irish warriors, Dürer made a study (now in the Graphische Sammlung Albertina, Vienna) of a 93-year-old man he met in Antwerp.[69]

In the sparsely populated Irish and Scottish countryside, some people managed to live long lives. Diarmit Ó Tuathail (O'Tool) was 80 when, in 1445, he led his followers in pursuit of a raiding party.[70] Aodh Ruadh Ó Domhnaill, ruler of Tír Conaill, was 73 when he was present at the Battle of Knockdoe;[71] Ruaidhri Mac Suibhne, galloglass chief of Fanad for 46 years, fought at Knockdoe when he was in his sixties.[72] The 10th Earl of Ormond died aged about 83 in 1614, despite a life of feuding and war; the 7th Earl of Desmond was probably around the same age when he died in 1462.[73]

Military training and participation in actual warfare could begin when Gaelic boys were very young, meaning some soldiers had service records of truly extraordinary length. An English report of the late 1400s explained that Irish 'sons learn to be men of war' from the age of 16.[74] Maybe this meant when real military service began (possibly first as a groom or harness-bearer) because the report describes the training not as a bit of fun now and then, but as skills 'continually practised.'[75] Irish children (perhaps not only the boys?) doubtless often knew the rudiments of fighting long before the age of 16. One source claims the sons of Irish nobles learned to ride and use weaponry from the age of seven.[76] If Diarmit Ó Tuathail actually was 80 in 1445, he might, therefore, have been weapons-trained for more than 70 years. Yet Ireland was not uniquely warlike here: the Statute of Winchester (1285) legislated that

Brooch (diameter 29.5mm) found at Trim, Co. Meath, and now in the National Museum of Ireland. Perhaps fourteenth or fifteenth century. (Drawing by Heather Cannan-Braniff)

---

69   See also his painting of his 70-year-old father in The National Gallery, London, and of the artist Michael Woglemut, aged somewhere around 82 in Germanisches Nationalmuseum, Nüremberg.
70   'O'Toole (Ó Tuathail), Feidhlim,' *DIB* (entry by E. O'Byrne).
71   'O'Donnell (Ó Domhnaill), Aodh Ruadh,' *DIB* (entry by E. O'Byrne).
72   Simms, 'Images of the Galloglass,' in Duffy, *World of the Galloglass*, p.112.
73   'Butler, Thomas,' *DIB* (entry by D. Edwards); 'Fitzgerald, James fitz Gerald,' *DIB* (entry by D. Beresford).
74   Quoted in Cannan, *Galloglass*, p.14.
75   Cannan, *Galloglass*, p.14.
76   D. McGettigan, *Red Hugh O'Donnell and the Nine Years' War* (Dublin: Four Courts Press, 2005), p.36.

all English males (and after 1308 all Irish males) between 15 and 60 should possess military equipment.[77]

Naturally, we must allow for clerical errors and people not knowing their exact age: the ages of two Mac Domhnaill galloglass captains are recorded in 1557 in the notes of an interview with the English as 50 'or thereabouts' and 70 'or thereabouts.'[78] But without a doubt we should picture old soldiers standing shoulder to shoulder with teenagers. There is nothing particularly Gaelic about this. The famous English knight William Marshal was around 70 at the battle of Lincoln in 1217 and the Earl of Surrey was 70 when he commanded the English army at Flodden in 1513.[79] Older soldiers were a part of armies across Europe during the medieval era, when armies were often formed out of family and feudal networks, from the willing and able regardless of their age, from those unable to escape the summons.

Irish children of the renaissance period. These combative youngsters are members of the Preston family a generation or two later than the anglophile Preston horseman illustrated in the colour plate section of the book. (Artwork by F. Cannan-Braniff)

Nor did the medieval mind have much of an idea of 'retirement'. It is also possible that some of the old were fitter and stronger than the aged of later periods. Perhaps, as well, the dreadful death toll from disease among the young meant there was less of a cult of youth than is the case today, and a stronger respect for experience, wisdom and the achievement of reaching an advanced age.

---

77 'Army,' *OCIH*.
78 H.F. Hore, 'The Rental Book of Gerald Fitzgerald, Ninth Earl of Kildare. Begun in the Year 1518,' *Journal of the Kilkenny and South-East of Ireland Archaeological Society*, new series, vol. 2, no. 2 (1859), p.276.
79 Asbridge, *Greatest Knight*, p.352; Niall Barr, *Flodden* (Stroud: Tempus, 2003), p.83.

4

'Natives'? 'Auxiliaries'? The Social & Cultural Character of Kern

Capitanus turbariorum Comitis Ormoniae ['Captain of the Earl of Ormond's raiders']

Inscription on the tomb of Edmund Purcell, St Canice's Cathedral.

As well as underestimating their military abilities, historians have ignored the diversity of ancestry and social status among kern, perpetuating a misleading image of kern as 'native' ruffians. We have mentioned Lee's portrait as an officer of kern but there is an earlier, less well-known image of a kern commander. It is not a portrait in the modern sense of the word but a stone tomb at St Canice's Cathedral, Kilkenny City. Carved in relief, the tomb commemorates Edmund Purcell, who died in 1549 having been a captain of the Earl of Ormond's kern. When referring to kern, modern writers (including Irish writers) slip into using language with worrying cultural overtones, calling kern 'auxiliaries' rather than 'soldiers,' implying professional inferiority and a lack of status as 'proper' soldiers. Occasionally Highlanders are called 'auxiliaries' by modern writers too, who likewise have a peculiar habit of referring to the Scottish nation as 'the Scots' as opposed to 'Scotland,' giving an impression of some sort of tribal 'race' rather than full nation state.

'Native' is another of the pejorative words used by historians when discussing kern, and yet nothing about Edmund Purcell's tomb or the Purcell family's origins supports the use of such a word. In 1544 Purcell led 100 kern for the 9th Earl of Ormond (Ormond's nephew commanding another 100) as part of Henry VIII's invasion of France.[1] One account says

---

1   Purcell Horan, 'Brief History,' pp.8–9.

THE GAELIC WORLD AT WAR: SOLDIERS & SOLDIERING IN IRELAND 1366–1547

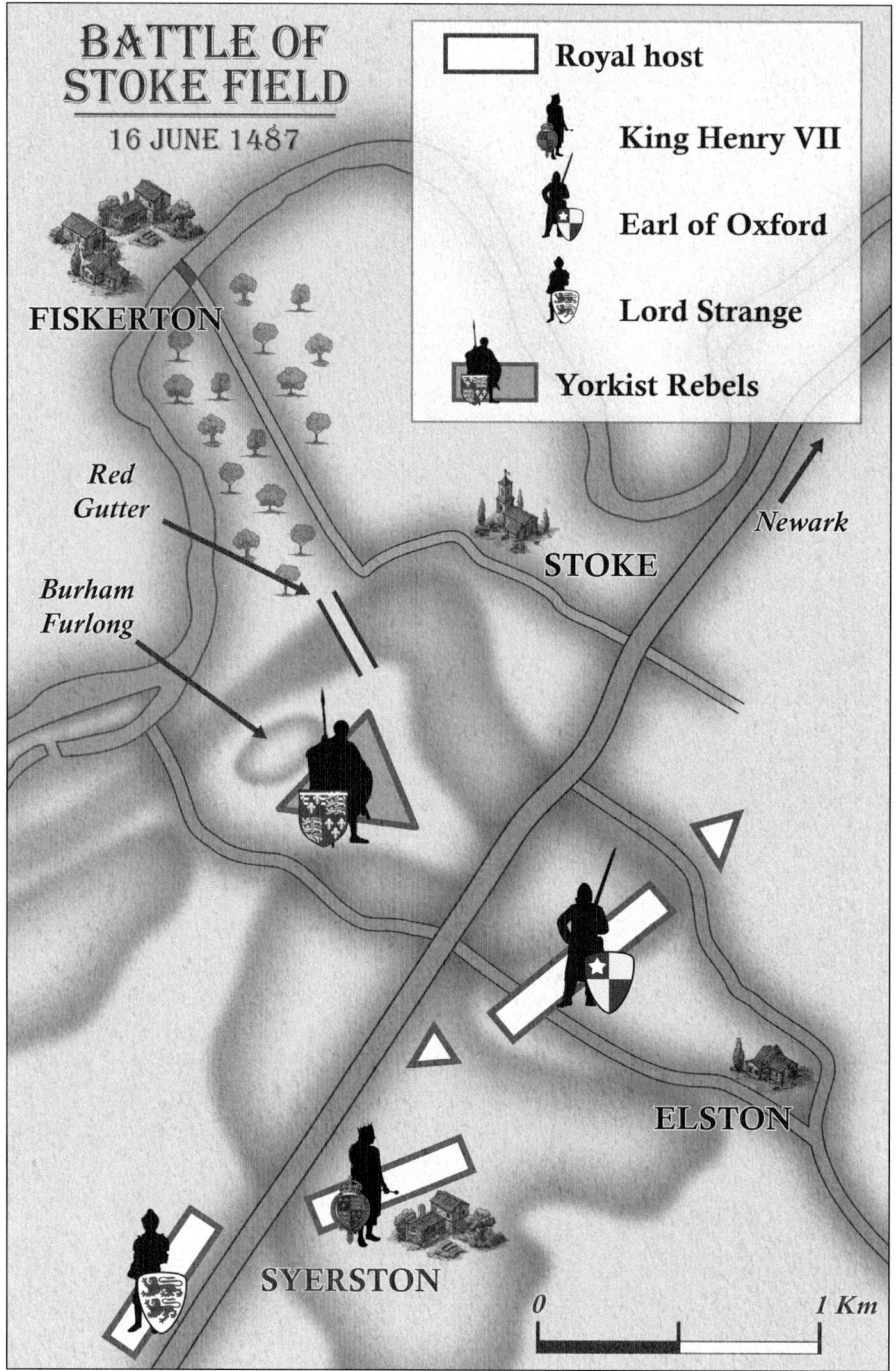

Crowned 'Edward VI' in Dublin at Christ Church Cathedral on 24th May 1487, Lambert Simnel was backed by a number of nobles including the 8th Earl of Kildare and the Earl of Lincoln. The crucial encounter came in England at Stoke (near Newark) on the 16th June 1487 when the Simnel army of Irish soldiers, English supporters and German, Swiss and Flemish mercenaries was defeated by Henry VII. The historian Michael Bennett suggested the rebel Simnel army (which Bennett estimated as less than 8,000 soldiers) may have been formed up as shown here: in a single block of infantry, possibly with some cavalry on the wings. The royal army, commanded by King Henry VII, the Earl of Oxford and Lord Strange, was much larger. Bennett hypothesises that the cream of Kildare's forces may have been left in Ireland. The Irish at Stoke, numbering perhaps 4,000, were commanded by Thomas Fitzgerald (brother of the Earl of Kildare); Thomas, a former chancellor of Ireland, perished in the battle along with many of his soldiers.

'NATIVES'? 'AUXILIARIES'? THE SOCIAL & CULTURAL CHARACTER OF KERN

Purcell's position as captain of kern in Ormond's army was hereditary,[2] another that he was Ormond's captain of galloglass.[3] The Purcells held their lands from the Ormond dynasty in return for military service, and may have been more general commanders of Ormond's forces than being merely responsible for kern. As well as unfortunate connotations of primitiveness, the word 'native' runs contrary to the fact that the Purcells came from England,[4] the name apparently coming from the French *pourcel* for 'little pig',[5] which probably accounts for the boars' heads in their heraldry.

Edmund Purcell's tomb shows a man in plate armour, mail coif or mantle and with a bowl-cut hairstyle. Above Purcell's head are the instruments of Christ's torment. The text around the tomb is Latin, not Irish, and is in Gothic script. The word 'Capitanus' (captain, head), and not some archaic 'Celtic' term, is used in Edmund's tomb inscription, as is 'turbariorum', an evocative Latin word which, in variant forms, meant kern.[6] Literally meaning disturbers or disorderly people, we can take it to mean something like harriers, raiders, reivers or assault force.

Although Purcell's tomb inscription identifies him as a commander of kern, the tomb sculptor represents him in mail and plate armour (indeed a distinct style of armour often seen on Irish tombs), not as a 'naked' kern. The portrayal is generic, but Purcell probably looked more like this – that is, in armour – when he participated in King Henry's invasion of France than some sort of Gaelic scarecrow in a dirty war-shirt. In the late sixteenth century the Crown deployed actual Englishmen such as Thomas Lee and Francis Cosby to lead units of Irish kern,[7] but before then kern officers (and no doubt some of their men) were people with less clearly defined 'Irish' or 'English' national identities. Edmund Purcell's tomb shows us neither an Englishman nor a 'native' living in a 'Celtic' bubble; what we see instead is a gentleman in heavy armour who has (and will no doubt try to use to his advantage) both Irish and English elements to his identity.

Nor does it appear Anglo-Irishmen became kern as part of any particular initiative; they had probably always been doing so. In 1537, an Edmund and William 'Purcer', described as 'brethren' (relatives, perhaps brothers or cousins), were 'captaygnes' of one of two 'companyes of kernes'

---

2 E. Hogan (ed.), *The Description of Ireland, and the State Thereof as it is at This Present in Anno 1598* (Dublin & London: M.H. Gill & Bernard Quaritch, 1878), p.68 n.i.
3 Purcell Horan, 'Brief History,' p.8.
4 E. MacLysaght, *Irish Families: Their Names, Arms & Origins*, 4th edn. (Blackrock: Irish Academic Press, 1991), p.139; MacLysaght, *Surnames*, p.249.
5 MacLysaght, *Irish Families*, p.139; MacLysaght, *Surnames*, p.249.
6 K. Simms in 'Gaelic Warfare in the Middle Ages,' in Bartlett & Jeffery, *Military History of Ireland*, p.100; Simms, *Kings to Warlords*, pp.121, 172.
7 Cannan, 'Generation of Villains,' p.30; Ellis, 'The Tudors,' in Bartlett & Jeffery, *Military History of Ireland*, pp.132–133, and C. Brady, 'The Captains' Games: Army and Society in Elizabethan Ireland', in Bartlett & Jeffery, *Military History of Ireland*, pp.153 & 156.

THE GAELIC WORLD AT WAR: SOLDIERS & SOLDIERING IN IRELAND 1366–1547

serving Piers Butler, 8th Earl of Ormond.[8] The same document states the other company of kern was captained by 'Jamys' and Robert 'Astyken', and alleges that the kern were moved around Butler's territories getting 'mete and drynke' for free from the locals (and when there was no meat – probably just meaning food – they would take money).[9] In the Victorian period the Rev. James Graves and Herbert J. Hore spotted that 'Astyken' is probably the surname Archdeacon.[10] If this is correct, we are again probably talking about Gaelicised Anglo-Irishmen rather than 'natives', because the Archdeacons of Kilkenny (the name sometimes became Cody) appear to have arrived from England as part of the 12th-century invasion of Ireland.[11] Like the Purcells in Tipperary, they held their lands towards the northern frontier of Ormond's domains, perhaps to act as a buffer.[12]

The O'Brien (or Ó Briain) manor of Leamaneh Castle in Co. Clare. (Drawing by F. Cannan-Braniff)

---

8   Hore & Graves, *Social State*, p.98.
9   Hore & Graves, *Social State*, p.98.
10 Hore & Graves, *Social State*, p.98 n.
11 M.M. Phelan, 'The Archedekins or MacCodys,' p.745 (published on the website of the Kilkenny Archaeological Society).
12 Maps in MacLysaght, *Surnames*, p.313, and MacLysaght, *Irish Families*, p.223.

The Keating Kern

Much of this picture of Gaelic-living Anglo-Irish gentry operating as kern is true of the Keatings, who became Ireland's best known kern. Although the Gaelicised version of their name, Céitinn, bears a resemblance to the ceithearn war-bands they commanded, the surname Keating was not originally Gaelic but probably Welsh, perhaps derived from the Welsh name Cethyn/Cethin/Gethin (possibly meaning dark or dusky).[13] A brief family tree for the Keatings of Baldwinstown (Wexford) is included in John O'Hart's *Irish Pedigrees*,[14] but it is unclear how the branches of Keatings in Wexford, Laois, Kildare and Tipperary (the famous historian Geoffrey Keating was born in Tipperary sometime around 1580) connect. An indication that they do all connect is that all the branches use the same coat of arms.[15]

It is said that the Keatings were a cadet branch of the Fitzgeralds who came to Ireland as part of the English and Welsh late 1100s land-grab.[16] The Keating arms appear to emphasise this ancestral link. The Earls of Kildare came to dominate Carlow, and the Keatings, along with the Mac Domhnaill galloglass, became the most important military unit in the Kildare army. The basis of the Keating shield is the Fitzgerald of Kildare's arms of argent a saltire gules to which the Keatings added four nettle leaves vert. Redmond Keating of Clonoghinthe in County Carlow, who died 1619, bore these arms,[17] and it is the Keatings of Carlow who became well known kern.

When 'Silken Thomas' rose in rebellion in the 1530s against Henry VIII, his captain of kern, William Keating, was captured by the English. Keating then offered to track down Thomas for the English.[18] Keating's motivations are unclear – had he genuinely turned on Thomas or was this a ruse? It does not seem to have been a genuine change of heart, given that the Keatings remained in Kildare service after the rising and that they were clearly very hostile to the English administration. It was alleged in 1566 that the 11th Earl of Kildare had '8 score ketynge kerne' maintained by coyne and livery in the borderlands of the English Pale.[19] The same report claimed the 11th Earl's Keatings did nothing useful for the Pale, being thieves that would guide enemies of English rule to the best places for raids and attacks.[20] It was further alleged that the Keatings were secretly opposed to English rule,

---

13 The name origin is suggested by MacLysaght, *Surnames*, p.171.
14 J. O'Hart, *Irish Pedigrees*, (Dublin: James Duffy & Co., 1892, 5th edn), vol. 2, p.271.
15 B. Burke, *The General Armory of England, Scotland, Ireland, and Wales* (Ramsbury: Heraldry Today, 1989), p.554.
16 MacLysaght, *Irish Families*, p.111; F. Cannan, 'Generation of Villains,' p.30.
17 National Library of Ireland: *Book of Funeral Entries*, vol. 3 (1604–1622), p.88.
18 'FitzGerald, Thomas ('Silken Thomas'), *DIB* (entry by M.A. Lyons).
19 Hore & Graves, *Social State*, p.170.
20 Hore & Graves, *Social State*, p.170.

THE GAELIC WORLD AT WAR: SOLDIERS & SOLDIERING IN IRELAND 1366–1547

and would threaten anyone who did not include the Earl of Kildare in their prayers.[21]

On the rare occasions historians mention the kern and galloglass who were hired to prop up the English administration in Ireland, they make it sound more organised and impressive than it really was. Some grand titles were bestowed (William Keating was styled 'Captain of the King's Kern' in 1546),[22] but the reality was that the Keatings were no Hibernian Yeoman of the Guard for England. Instead Keatings were hired in small numbers by the government as and when needed as part of stingily funded taskforces. They joined the hunt for Shane O'Neill in Ulster in the 1560s.[23] A worn letter dated 1575 and addressed to 'The Right Honorable the L:[ord] Burghley High Thresaror of England' contains 'keatinges declaraton' and a note about 'The victuallers suddeyn departure.'[24] Keatings were again in government service in 1588.[25]

Never do the Keating kern appear to have been enthusiastic supporters of English expansion in Ireland. In the library of Lambeth Palace is a report, probably made around 1600, evaluating the loyalty to the English Crown

Irish society – or, at least, how chiefs and their privileged inner circle saw Irish society. (Drawing by F. Cannan-Braniff)

---

21   Hore & Graves, *Social State*, p.175.
22   Cannan, 'Hags,' p.16.
23   Cannan, 'Hags,' p.16.
24   NA SP 63/51/42.
25   Cannan, 'Hags,' p.16.

of leading Irish families. The Keatings were considered important enough to be included in the report, and despite the fact they had worked with English authorities in the past, the attitude of the 'ketings kern' was that they were 'ylle [ill] disposed' to the government '& now Rebells'.[26] Like many of the galloglass, there was a degree of political consistency to their actions. Although those attitudes might be masked under double-dealing and short-term alliances with the English and others, the Keatings were very much a traditional Anglo-Irish family: Catholic, Gaelicised, landed, factional, and with the stirrings of something beginning to resemble love of nation and homeland.

Social Standing of the Ordinary Kern

If kern captains came from old families, what about the ordinary kern? In early Ireland, having a degree of wealth and status meant you served as a soldier. In later medieval Ireland it was increasingly the other way around: being a soldier gave you status and power over the community, regardless of origins. Ireland had a large population of very poor agricultural workers who traditionally did not serve as soldiers.[27] The kern lived like kings compared to this great mass of people. However lowly his origins, becoming a kern gave a man considerable power, being something of a licence to behave badly and demand free food and hospitality from the local community.

Even hostile English legislation in 1541 aimed at limiting traditional Irish dress recognised elements of Gaelic precedence, allowing most fabric for the shirts of Irish lords or nobles, followed by those of horsemen and vassals, and then by kern and Scots (whether this means galloglass as well as redshanks is unclear). But the fact that the 1541 act permitted still shorter lengths of cloth for the shirts of servants and (even shorter) for the shirts of labourers reminds us that the kern was some rungs up from the bottom of the Gaelic social ladder.[28]

In other words, it is inaccurate to consider kern 'working class'. Kern may well have often brought servants with them to clean their equipment and weapons and cook their meals. Unlike soldiers of later periods, kern would not have been expected to spend hours mopping floors, cleaning latrines, going through drills, painting walls and making beds. Nor do they appear to have worn uniforms (though one wonders if some of them wore family colours or liveries). The 'military revolution' increased the size of armies, but it worsened conditions for the private soldier. Punishments could be brutal,[29] but the ordinary medieval Gaelic soldier, often something of a 'gentleman ranker', appears to have been treated with a great deal more

---

26   Carew Ms 621, f.107r.
27   Ellis, *Ireland*, p.44.
28   Dunlevy, *Dress ain Ireland*, p.54.
29   For example, see Cannan, *Galloglass*, p.30.

respect by his commanders than ordinary soldiers in the Wehrmacht, the Roman Army, Frederick the Great's army or other forces which historians admire so much for their 'effectiveness.' Meeting a rank-and-file kern, galloglass, redshank or horseman would probably have been more like meeting a high-caste Indian serving as a 'sepoy' than, say, a press-ganged sailor of Nelson's day or a Napoleonic period redcoat who had taken the King's shilling to escape poverty and hunger.

5

Out of the Shadows: Reconstructing the Daltinne & Gairm Shluaigh Fighter

>...if the chieftains themselves, with mortal hatred, hold an enmity against someone, they do not make the night the tool of their plundering; rather they get together an army of murderers, raiders and a rabble of the servant class and in broad daylight they plunder the goods of their enemy.
>
> Stanihurst, *Great Deeds in Ireland*

The hardcore of Gaelic military forces used by chiefs as guardsmen and enforcers – kern, galloglass, horsemen and redshanks – were an elite and were by no means the only people found in Irish armies.

Historians have traditionally attributed the collapse of Irish uprisings, whether the Bruce invasion in the 1300s or Desmond's struggle with Elizabeth in the late 1500s, to chronic in-fighting and lack of political unity. This is undeniably an important reason. However, there may be another reason which has gone undetected – namely, that far from everyone in Irish armies was a professional fighter. For accompanying the kern, galloglass, horsemen and redshanks were large numbers of servants, camp followers and conscripted tenantry. In this respect Irish armies were similar to other medieval armies. However, the presence in Irish armies of these support troops and part-time warriors has gone unnoticed by historians, even though at times they must have constituted a very considerable proportion of a chief's army, possibly outnumbering the galloglass, kern and other professionals, and making the army look and feel more impressive than it really was.

Historians speak of the 'small scale' of Irish warfare. In reality, Irish armies were by no means always small. Creton heard it reported that Art

THE GAELIC WORLD AT WAR: SOLDIERS & SOLDIERING IN IRELAND 1366–1547

Head of an agricultural tool found at Prospect, Limerick, in 1947 (total length 29.6cm). One can easily imagine such a tool being wielded as an improvised weapon by the poorest members of an Irish farming community. (Limerick Museum)

Mór Mac Murchadha, de facto King of Leinster, had 'three thousand hardy men' to be used against Richard II's invasion force in 1399.[1] Being a land under one monarch, it was easier for England to field large armies than Ireland; Richard II had arrived in Ireland in 1399 with perhaps as many as 9,000–10,000 soldiers.[2] But raising armies was not the problem for Irish commanders; the problem was keeping those armies from fragmenting. In 1535, Silken Thomas, 10th Earl of Kildare, attacked Dublin with around 15,000 men. Within months his force dwindled to no more than 100 cavalry, 300 infantry and 10 handgunners.[3] The 15th Earl of Desmond was said to have raised 5,000 men in 1560 for war with Ormond,[4] but, as mentioned above, by his death in 1583 he had only a few loyal followers left.

Plummeting numbers were partly due to deaths from combat, assassination and execution. The Earl of Ormond told Elizabeth I that between December 1579 to mid-1581 his forces had killed 5,650 rebels, servants and followers allied to Desmond.[5] Double-dealing and the lure of honourable terms of surrender from the enemy were, however, more serious problems. Still, desertion rates do not appear to have been even across units. Silken Thomas had gone to Dublin in 1534 with a force of up to 1,000 soldiers, including a guard of 140 smart horsemen (the silk fringes on their headwear giving Thomas his nickname).[6] It is eminently possible that the 100 horsemen who remained loyal to Thomas during his rebellion were the survivors of that 140-strong guard.

Daltinnes & Logistical Support

Irish horsemen were the highest status soldiers – but what of the lowest rungs on the military ladder? Stanihurst says the lowest rank in the Irish scale of military precedence were 'daltinnes', who ranked below kern.[7] Stanihurst explains daltinnes as 'runners' and 'lightarmed servants, or footmen,' who acted as grooms and as light skirmishers using javelins, fighting without armour.[8]

Gaelic commanders clearly understood the value of logistical support, since their armies had an array of people in support roles. Stanihurst refers to the wounded Irish soldiers being carried home on an 'eight-man litter,' with treatment being provided by hereditary physicians. He mocks these

---

1   Quoted in McGettigan, *Richard II*, p.169.
2   McGettigan, *Richard II*, p.168.
3   Lyons, 'FitzGerald, Thomas,' *DIB*.
4   'Fitzgerald, Gerald fitz James,' *DIB* (entry by A. M. McCormack).
5   'Butler, Thomas,' *ODNB* (entry by D. Edwards).
6   Lyons, 'FitzGerald, Thomas,' *DIB*; Ellis, 'Fitzgerald, Thomas,' *ODNB*.
7   Stanihurst, *Great Deeds*, p.125.
8   Stanihurst, *Great Deeds*, pp.125–127.

Gaelic 'empiricks,' but, whether skilled or useless, the presence of medical staff demonstrates that medical aid was at least given consideration.[9]

The Comyn Folke

Traditionally, local tenantry had been the mainstay of a chief's army. 'Tradition' is of course in the eye of the beholder, and it is not impossible that early Irish communal levies included women. Historians have shown no interest in the role of women in medieval Irish armies. Yet we know there were some very forceful women in medieval Ireland (the landowner Roesia de Verdun, d. 1247, for instance), and it would be extraordinary if medieval Irishwomen were militarily inactive.[10] St Adomnán's 'Law of the Innocents' (which attempted to protect civilians in war and was enacted by an assembly Irish of nobles and clergy in or around 697 CE 'as an everlasting law until Doom'), claims Irishwomen went 'into battle and battlefield, into encounter and encampment, expedition and hosting, wounding and slaughter.'[11] Possibly – for the situation is far from clear – Adomnán's 'Law' led to a reworking in Ireland of compulsory military service to include only able-bodied adult males, a system that became known as *gairm shluaigh* (*gairm*: call on, proclaim; *shulaigh*: people, multitude) or *coimhéirghe* ('rising out,' obligation to serve).[12]

During the late Middle Ages, the composition of Irish armies shifted again, this time from all-male local conscripts to permanently retained professional soldiers and hired mercenaries. This change also occurred in England. Both in Ireland and England there remained an assumption, however, that the local tenantry would assist their lord in time of war.[13] An anonymous Anglo-Irish writer reported around 1515 that the biggest Irish army they knew of 'passe not 500 sperys [spear-armed cavalry] 500 galloglasseis and 1000 kerne'; but twice the throwaway reference to 'besyde

---

9   Stanihurst, *Great Deeds*, p.127.
10 There were also some very forceful women in early modern Ireland including the pirate-queen Gráinne O'Malley, the landowner 'Red Mary' O'Brien, and the Highland aristocrat Agnes Campbell. My painting of Red Mary can be seen in Cannan, 'Machiavellian Mercenaries?'
11 G. Márkus (trans. and ed.), *Adomnán's 'Law of the Innocents'* (Kilmartin House Trust, 2008; published online by eprints.gla.ac.uk), pp.2, 10, 16.
12 MacLennan, *Pronouncing and Etymological Dictionary*, *gairm* and *sluagh*; Simms's glossary in *Kings to Warlords*, pp.174–175; C. Mackay, *The Auld Scots Dictionary* (Glasgow: Lang Syne, 2002), 'slogan.'
13 For instance, the Percy Army at the skirmish at Heworth in 1453 included hundreds of yeomen and husbandmen (surely Percy tenants), and in the Napoleonic age, the head of the Percy family, the Duke of Northumberland, was able to retain a 1,500-strong defence force known as the Percy Tenantry Volunteers. Similarly, Leonard Dacre raised 3,000 tenants for use against the Crown in 1570: Gillingham, *Wars of the Roses*, p.33; Ellis, 'Tudor Borderlands,' in Morrill, *Oxford Illustrated History*, p.71.

THE GAELIC WORLD AT WAR: SOLDIERS & SOLDIERING IN IRELAND 1366-1547

Head of a crude polearm, possibly adapted from agricultural tool. Painted lettering says it was found in Ireland; perhaps seventeenth century or a relic from the 1798 rising. (Somerset County Council Heritage Service)

the comyn folke' is included, who presumably could be called on in an emergency.[14] A survey commissioned by England in 1597 of the domains of Donal MacCarthy Mór, 26th MacCarthy Mór, defined *Garemsloaeg* as 'a rising upon a warning given of all the able men,' each man being expected to bring a 'sufficient weapon and three dayes victuals' on pain of a fine of a 'choyce cowe or xxs old money' for non-attendance.[15] The survey also says, however, that some people defied the muster and the 'fyne.'[16]

No doubt the assembled recruits, as tough rural men, made a threatening show for a one-off raid or short clash with the enemy. Some modern writers get carried away when they read of the fighting skills of medieval knights, and make wild claims that knights, well trained and snug in their armour, had next to nothing to fear from peasants. This overlooks the fact that fighting skills existed among the poor of Ireland, England and Scotland, based around fighting with such implements as staffs and cudgels. But whether self-defence techniques could sustain a force of rural poor for long on the battlefield is another question. They cannot have had the same tactical knowledge as the professionals, and perhaps these were the poorly armed 'naked' men the English thought were kern. Some may have felt a deep loyalty to their chief (chiefs like the Desmond and Ormond earls seem to have been genuinely popular with their tenantry), but others may well have felt they had little to gain from participating in wars where the only real aim was to achieve regional supremacy over rival chiefs.

Private Armies in Ireland

The remedy to the unreliability of the 'rising out' was to garrison your lands with professional soldiers. It is not always easy to distinguish the permanently employed household soldiers from the troops supplied only in wartime by allies or vassal families, or from the muster of local semi-professionals. Despite the professionalising of Irish warfare, every chief would remain reliant on the traditional levy of local men and the short-term hiring of mercenaries if they wanted an army bigger than about 1,000 soldiers.

---

14   Quoted in Simms, *Kings to Warlords*, p.126.
15   'The Desmond Survey,' published online at CELT.
16   'The Desmond Survey,' published online at CELT; Simms, *Kings to Warlords*, pp.142–143.

RECONSTRUCTING THE DALTINNE & GAIRM SHLUAIGH FIGHTER

The 10th Earl of Ormond, one of Ireland's strongest magnates, had a private army of 1,000 or so men.[17] Shane O'Neill, who also had significant regional power, is said to have been always guarded by 600 armed men.[18] The 8th Earl of Kildare, who died in 1513 and was, in the words of S. B. Chrimes 'the real King of Ireland,'[19] had a permanent personal retinue of about 120 galloglass and 120 kern, and he could call on others when needed.[20]

Around 1600, the army of Ó Domhnaill of Tír Conaill, the most powerful individual in North-West Ireland, included 'sixty horsemen' and '120 foot soldiers' (both provided by Ó Dochartaigh, or O'Doherty, of Inishowen), and 300 Mac Suibhne 'Gallowglasses with armour' (120 'sent to the field' from 'MacSweeny Fanad,' 120 from 'MacSweeny na Doe,' 60 from 'MacSweeny Baghaineach').[21] Presumably this is excluding galloglass servants since we are told in the document that the totals are for galloglass 'with armour,' it being noted of the Fanad galloglass that 'should any of them want armour' Mac Suibhne Fanad was 'to give a beef in lieu of it.'[22] If each galloglass had just one servant, that would be 600 mouths to feed and house. Some of the demand would have been met by the goods the document lists as tribute from sub-chiefs to Ó Domhnaill. Fanad had to give 18 'Beeves', 10 'milch cows, and 10 marks for the support of Bonaghts.'[23] Aodh Ruadh (Red Hugh) Ó Domhnaill's steward, 'who was living an old man in the time of James I A.D. 1626,' recollected Mac Suibhne Tír Boghaine had to give '18 Beeves,' probably three times a year.[24]

Even with these supplies coming in, it was an extraordinary drain on the local economy, showing what a compulsion war was for the nobility. One suspects these paper figures of galloglass and others are optimistic tallies of when, or if, units reached their intended strength. Permanent Irish garrisons could be surprisingly small. But population levels were also small, meaning it was possible for just a few soldiers and their servants to stamp their authority on the local area. The Mac Domhnaills of Tinnakill received a confirmation of their lands from Charles I stipulating that, ordinarily, the Mac Domhnaills only need maintain two fully-equipped horsemen 'of the English nation and blood' and 'duodecim habiles Securigers, Anglice vocat. "Galloglasses".'[25] Or in translation – '12 skilled axe-men, called in

---

17 'Butler, Thomas,' *DIB* (entry by D. Edwards).
18 Hayes-McCoy, *Irish Battles*, p.76.
19 S. B. Chrimes, *Henry VII* (New Haven & London: Yale University Press, 1999), p.75.
20 Ellis, 'The Tudors,' p.120; F. Cannan, 'England's Irish Warriors,' *Military Illustrated*, no. 255 (Aug. 2009), p.34; Hayes-McCoy, *Irish Battles*, p.58.
21 RIA Miscellaneous O'Donovan Ms 14/B/7, p.423.
22 RIA Miscellaneous O'Donovan Ms 14/B/7, p.423.
23 RIA Miscellaneous O'Donovan Ms 14/B/7, p.423.
24 RIA Miscellaneous O'Donovan Ms 14/B/7, p.424.
25 J. Huband Smith, 'Letters Patent of James Mac Donnell', *Ulster Journal of Archaeology*, 2 (1854), pp.123-124. In August 2009 the Earl of Antrim and the Hon.

THE GAELIC WORLD AT WAR: SOLDIERS & SOLDIERING IN IRELAND 1366–1547

English "Galloglasses". The document is essentially a reissue of a grant the Mac Domhnaill family received from Elizabeth I, and there is no evidence galloglass existed in any shape or form in the days of Charles I. But the document preserves the old expectation that, if summoned by the Lord Deputy, the Mac Domhnaills should bring every armed servant and tenant they can muster, and to give their followers provisions for three days.[26]

As well as summoning servants and tenants, chiefs could also hire mercenaries on temporary contracts. The constables and marshals in Gaelic retinues appear to have been not only field commanders, but officials responsible for sourcing troops; perhaps this included the hiring of mercenaries. It was claimed the Earl of Ormond, one of Ireland's greatest magnates, was able to assemble no less than 800 galloglass in 1539, although this might include harness-bearers and attendants.[27] In 1512 Aodh Dubh Ó Domhnaill of Tír Chonaill hired an astonishing 1,500 axemen in Fermanagh and north Connacht, Darren McGettigan seeing in this a possible influence of the Italian *condotta* system (Ó Domhnaill having made a pilgrimage to Rome in 1510–1511).[28]

Stanihurst records that in the 1540s the 9th Earl of Ormond 'leuyed [levied] of hys Tenauntes and Reteynours' 600 'Gallowglasses,' as well as 400 'Kearnes,' 'three score' horsemen, and 440 'shot' for use against Scotland.[29] Many of these men were no doubt part of Ormond's full-time private army. Yet Stanihurst tells us Ormond mustered this force on a green near Dublin. Given they had to muster, and that, Stanihurst says, they 'tooke shypping' only after the troops were provided 'wyth Munition and victualles,'[30] this was clearly not a force that Ormond, rich and powerful as he was, had at his disposal all the time.

Painted wooden statue of St Catherine of Alexandria, probably late fifteenth century, from the Kilcorban Third Order Dominican Priory. Although the overall look of the statue is similar to that of northern European sculpture of the period, note that this figure has an Irish-looking ring brooch, suggesting the figure was made by an Irish sculptor. (Collection of Clonfert Diocesan Museum. Artwork by F. Cannan-Braniff)

Hector McDonnell told me that this document (essentially a re-issue of document to the Tinnakill Mac Domhnaills from Elizabeth I) appears to have vanished, but it might now be in Australia.

26   Smith, 'Letters Patent,' pp.123–124.
27   Lydon, 'Scottish Soldier Abroad,' in Duffy, *Robert the Bruce's Irish Wars*, p.105.
28   See Mac Eiteagáin, 'Renaissance and the Late Medieval Lordship of Tír Chonaill,' in Nolan, Ronayne & Dunlevy, *Donegal*, pp.203–228.
29   Stanihurst, *Irish Chronicle*, p.303.
30   Stanihurst, *Irish Chronicle*, p.303.

Conclusions

A Gaelic commander would no doubt have felt pleased that Vegetius believed peasants make good soldiers because they are tough. But Vegetius meant peasants become good soldiers once they have been properly trained and equipped.[31] Once one starts thinking about MacCarthy Mór's followers with their 'sufficient' weapons – perhaps sometimes no more than spears, javelins, flails, slings and knives (though some might have had access to castle armouries) – one can see why Irish chiefs, like the nobility elsewhere in Europe, switched during the late Middle Ages from a reliance on sprawling levies of tenants to a reliance on full-time professional soldiers. This short-term military solution would, though, stunt serious growth and diversification in the Gaelic Irish economy.

---

31 Vegetius, *De Re Militari*, p.16.

6

Redshanks as Marines

Chan'eil fhios ciod an claidheamh a bhios 'san truaill gus an táirnear e

(It is not known what sword is in the sheath till it is drawn)
Scots Gaelic proverb

He looks like a Lochaber axe.

Scots English proverb, dating from at least the first half of the seventeenth century

The nation that Irish chiefs looked to most for additional military personnel was Scotland. Probably for centuries, Scots had been an integral part of the Irish military system, but historians have been similarly damning about medieval Scottish equipment, tactics and ability in set-piece battles. And yet, Scottish armies (occasionally with a little French help) defeated English armies in battle in 1297, 1303, 1307, 1314, 1319, 1388, 1421, 1448 and 1545. Scots, many of them Gaelic-speakers (indeed, some of the differences between medieval 'lowland' and 'highland' Scotland have been grossly overstated), likewise performed very well in all but the final battle of Edward Bruce's 1315–1318 invasion of Ireland. In other words, a re-analysis of Gaelic Scottish military competency is demanded.

'Redshanks' or Highlanders were nothing new in late medieval Irish armies, but possibly the demand for their military skills grew from about the end of the 1400s. They were available in large numbers, had their own transport, were first-rate sailors and soldiers, and had their own armour and equipment (much of which was excellent).[1] The term 'redshank', denoting

---

[1] For positive assessments (as opposed to the usual denigrating descriptions) of Highland battle-dress see D. H. Caldwell, 'Having the Right Kit: West Highlanders Fighting in Ireland,' in Duffy, *World of the Galloglass*, pp.144–168; and Cannan,

REDSHANKS AS MARINES

During the Nine Years' War, a Mac Suibhne chieftain escaped from an English ship by swimming. (Artwork by F. Cannan-Braniff)

the ruddy bare legs of Highlanders, was not meant as a compliment. When we say 'redshanks,' or 'New Scots' as they were called, we are referring to warriors from Scotland's Highlands and Islands, but we should possibly include medieval Galloway (often forgotten about as a Gaelic region). When it comes to Scottish soldiers who were drawn through cultural affinity and self-interest to Ireland, we should think of these 'redshanks' as western Scots – the key divide in Scotland when it came to feeling a connection with Ireland was east–west, not north–south.

Naval Power

We earlier invited you to consider galloglass as being like marines because marines are a famously dependable elite. But redshanks and the first generations of galloglass were literally marines. Used to riding the choppy waters of the Irish Sea in their galleys, they became adept at conducting hit-and-run raids using shallow-draught galleys which, using oars as well as sails, were ideally suited for quick entry and departure from the point of landing. These skills had existed before the Middle Ages, and they did not

---

Scottish Arms and Armour.

die with the Middle Ages. Martin recounts that what he calls the chief's *'guard de corps'* of old were 'well trained in managing the sword and target,' wrestling, swimming, jumping, dancing and archery, and that they were 'were stout seamen.'[2]

Dynasties all along the Scottish West Coast (and not just north of the 'Highland line') were capable of pooling their resources for larger scale operations. The 1315 Bruce invasion of Ireland opened with perhaps as many as 6,000 men being landed on the Antrim coast. Bearing in mind that Scotland's population must have been less than a million, this medieval 'Operation Overlord' would have required an immense amount of intelligence gathering, reconnaissance, knowledge of tides and reading of weather conditions. Many of the ships were supplied by the Mac Domhnaill and Mac Ruaidhri clans.[3] And yet the value of naval forces does not seem to have rubbed off on the Irish chiefs who, with a few exceptions, remained largely land-orientated in their thinking about war.[4] But the draw for redshanks was that the Irish lords had a wealth that the Hebridean lairds generally lacked.[5]

As well as ships and soldiers, the Bruce invasion force deployed what can only be seen as 'pan-Gaelic' propaganda to rally Irish fighters to a Scottish (or anti-English) cause. Bruce forces proceeded to beat armies loyal to England (not all Englishmen by any means) at Connor (inland west of Larne) in September 1315, apparently at Kells in December 1315, and at Skerries (near Ardscull) in January 1316 when an Anglo-Irish army was beaten, in winter (note that medieval warfare was not restricted to summer as many believe), by a smaller Bruce force.[6] The picture is therefore pretty clear: medieval Scotland was highly proficient in warfare, a strength underpinned by a fairly durable national unity – something Ireland did not have.

Swimming

Further evidence of thoroughness of training for amphibious warfare is the fact that some Gaelic soldiers – perhaps many – could swim. Across different

---

2   Martin, *Description*, pp.78–79. In the same passage Martin calls this bodyguard 'gentlemen,' implying – as does the presence of dancing in the list of required skills – that louts were not wanted; the bodyguard should have strength, commitment and skill, but also a bit of social polish and grace.
3   C. McNamee, *The Wars of the Bruces: Scotland, England and Ireland, 1306–1328* (Phantassie: Tuckwell, 1997), p.170; S. Duffy, 'The Bruce Invasion of Ireland: A Revised Itinerary and Chronology,' in Duffy, *Robert the Bruce's Irish Wars*.
4   Ellis, *Ireland*, p.250.
5   Ellis, *Ireland*, p.250.
6   McNamee, *Wars of the Bruces*, chap. 5; Duffy, 'Bruce Invasion,' esp. pp.10–25; Lydon, 'Scottish Soldier Abroad' in Duffy, *Robert the Bruce's Irish Wars*, pp.92–93 & 95; Cannan, *Galloglass*, p.48.

cultures, swimming was considered a useful skill for soldiers to learn, possibly before it became a civilian sport.[7] Vegetius said soldiers should be taught to swim, advice repeated by Pisan, and More's Utopian soldiers practice 'swimming in armour' – if you think that sounds impossible you might consider the fact that swimming in armour was one of the martial arts of the samurai, an activity still performed today.[8]

Swimming keeps you fit (especially if you do it in armour), washes your body, and swimming in the sea off Scotland and Ireland will certainly hone that hardness of body and spirit that medieval writers like Loutfut spoke of. Some Gaels were evidently strong swimmers; in the Nine Years' War, Maol Mhuire Mac Suibhne, last Lord of Na Tuatha, escaped (aided by a prostitute) from an English ship on the Foyle by jumping into the water and swimming to safety, enabling him to live to fight another day.[9]

Home-spun Wisdom or Professional Instruction?

If all these skills existed in Scotland and Ireland, how did soldiers learn them? It is true that in the premodern Gaeltacht crafts often passed from one generation to the next, sometimes for centuries, and often in the service of chiefs. It appears much education took place within the family or foster families, one generation passing on their skills to the next. Many Gaelic warriors would have learned their skills this way. However, one wonders if military professionals like redshanks and the famous galloglass families offered more professional styles of instruction, and perhaps even training schools for their recruits.

Stanihurst contends kern loved their swords but had 'no familiarity with the art of the fencing schools.'[10] We do know there were fencing masters in early modern Ireland,[11] so is this necessarily true of all kern? Perhaps swordfighting skills were no longer common by Stanihurt's time.[12] At any rate, weapons skills remained as strong as ever in the Scottish Highlands. While the medieval evidence is lacking, it is said that there was at some point a 'fencing school' at, or near, Glenuig in the Highlands, that the Stewarts of Ardshiel kept a school for swordsmanship in the seventeenth and early

---

7 B. Tsui, *Why We Swim* (London: Penguin, 2020), pp.155–156.
8 Vegetius, *De Re Militari*, p.21; Pisan, *Book of Fayttes*, pp.35–36; More, *Utopia*, p.97; Tsui, *Why We Swim*, chap. 14.
9 R. Bagwell, *Ireland Under the Tudors* (London: Longmans, Green & Co., 1890), vol. 3, p.375; Gillespie, 'Gaelic Families,' in Nolan, Ronayne & Dunlevy, *Donegal*, p.784.
10 Stanihurst, *Great Deeds*, p.125.
11 D. Miller, *Irish Swordsmanship: Fencing and Duelling in Eighteenth Century Ireland* (New York: Hudson Society, 2017), esp. chap. 5.
12 Even if old skills were being lost, Garret Barry (who died in 1646) thought the Irish of his day still had an affinity for sword and shield-fighting and so should 'frequente the sworde and target': *Discourse*, p.9.

eighteenth centuries, and that chiefs of Lovat trained their men how to fight.[13] One suspects such places had existed in the medieval Highlands as well. One of the principal strengths of Highlanders was that they knew their military craft, and perhaps part of the appeal of Highlanders for Irish recruiters was not just that they had the skills, but that they could share those skills with Irish soldiers.

---

13 H. Cheape, 'Clanranald's Blacksmith,' *Clan Donald Magazine*, no. 12 (1991).

7

Marcshlua: The 'Knights' of A Gaelic Army

> The Irish Hobby is a pretty fine horse …. Nimble, light, pleasant and apt to be taught. …. Yea and the Irish men both with darts and with light spears use to skirmish with them in the field. And many of them do prove to that use very well by means they be so light and swift.
>
> *The Four Chief Offices Belongyng to Horsemanshippe* by the Englishman Thomas Blundeville (1522?-1606?)

Adam Loutfut's advice in his late fifteenth century Scots version of Vegetius was that country people make the best infantry and nobles make the best cavalry.[1] Leaders of Irish armies had long followed this principle. The prestige enjoyed by cavalry stems from the fact that horses are expensive to own and care for and are therefore status symbols. Whereas the Bishop of Chester's galloglass axe was valued at 2 shillings in 1597, horses sold during the same period less than 50 miles away at Shrewsbury fetched 40 to 50 shillings each.[2] It was said in 1399 that Art Mór Mac Murchadha, rode a horse costing 400 cows.[3] If the kern was a pawn on a chessboard, the galloglass was a rook, and the horseman was a knight. Like a knight, an Irish cavalryman commanded his own small unit of grooms with spare mounts, it being reported in 1566 that the Earl of Kildare's cavalry had two 'boyes' for every horse.'[4]

---

1   Quoted in Allmand, *The De Re Militari*, p.236.
2   M. Campbell, *The English Yeoman Under Elizabeth and the Stuarts* (London: Merlin, 1983), p.206.
3   McGettigan, *Richard II*, p.81.
4   Hore & Graves, *Social State*, p.168.

Irish Cavalry Harness

When it comes to equipment, conventional wisdom classifies the Irish *marcshlua* or cavalry as light horsemen who held their lances overarm rather than underarm and did not use stirrups. Only the last of these claims is straightforwardly true: as far as we know, only foreigners and the most anglicised of horse riders used stirrups in Ireland.

The other claims require more explanation. Most Irish cavalry were certainly lightly equipped, mounted on relatively small 'hobbies,' from which comes the term 'hobelar' for a light horseman. Robin Frame calculated that in Anglo-Irish armies, the light horse on average outnumbered the heavy horse by a ratio of nearly 5 to 1.[5] Heavy cavalry were, then, a rarity in Ireland, and probably often Englishmen.

However, the 'lightness' of Irish cavalry has been exaggerated. In 1549 the portreeve and burgesses of Wexford appealed to the English authorities for protection from 'Gharne' (kern) and 'Horsemen, in cumpled harness, whell apuntthid' (in complete harness, well appointed).[6] 'Harness' was a term for armour, and 'well appointed' usually meant well-equipped, and thus it sounds like these Irish horsemen were in complete armour or were at the very least heavily equipped.

Depictions of Irish cavalry of the 1300s to *c*. 1600 suggest they were about as heavily armoured as a Norman knight, minus the stirrups. Or, put another way, as heavily armoured as a galloglass on horseback. Historians cite stock descriptions of Irish horsemen from Stanihurst, Dymmok et al, but the evidence from art suggests a wider, and less exclusively Gaelic range of cavalry equipment was used in Ireland. Henry VIII's officials pardoned a Peter Walshe, who they were unsure if he was a 'horseman or kern,'[7] and we actually have an image of a late medieval Walsh (a surname, along with variant forms including Welsh, usually considered in Ireland to indicate descent from someone Welsh) horseman. Published in 1823, the image is of a sculpture of a horseman. The sculpture itself, which from the style of armour could be as old as the 1370s or 1380s, appears to have been at Piltown Protestant church but is now lost. The horseman carries a shield bearing the three arrowheads of the Walsh family.[8]

Some aspects of the Walsh figure are characteristically Irish. The figure wears the usual protective mix favoured by galloglass, horsemen and redshanks: open-faced helmet, mail and quilting, and no leg armour. But, as with Edmund Purcell's tomb, there are also details suggesting contact

---

5   'Hobelar,' *OCIH* (entry by K. Simms).
6   Hore & Graves, *Social State*, p.38.
7   Quoted in Cannan, 'Hags of Hell,' p.15.
8   P. Harbison, 'An Illustration of the Lost Walsh Knight from the Jerpoint Cloister Arcade' (published on the website of the Kilkenny Archaeological Society); Burke, *General Armory*, pp.1069–1070.

with the outside world.⁹ Walsh's shield is heater-shaped, not the round Gaelic targe-type shield, and it is possible he is wearing a neck guard of scale armour. Rather than the classic Irish *scian*, Walsh appears to carry a baselard with an H-shaped grip, a type of dagger one associates with England and 'mainstream' Europe in the age of Chaucer and the Hundred Years War.

Social Status

Henry VIII's officials were also unsure whether Walsh was a 'gent.' or 'yeoman.'¹⁰ That uncertainty over Walsh's social status and whether he was a kern or horseman (supposedly distinct rungs on the military ladder of precedence) suggest we should not be rash in concluding that all Irish cavalry were nobles. English medieval and early modern armies had many wealthy nobles in their heavy cavalry, but among their light cavalry, mounted archers and hobelars were men from the minor gentry and yeomanry – men from the blurred boundary where noble status blurred into that of respectable freeholder. The crucial difference is that Gaels did not feel they needed knighthoods, official recognition, or bits of parchment entitling them to coats of arms or titles in order to feel noble. Being a gentleman or gentlewoman in Gaelic society came largely from ancestry and preserving family tradition. 'I've been dubbed to my liking' says the Scots warrior Fergus of Galloway (loosely based on the real ruler of Galloway of that name) in Guillaume le Clerc's Old French tale.¹¹ An Irishman would have instantly understood the sentiment.

Carving on a Butler tomb at Gowran, Co. Kilkenny of Christ displaying His wounds; early sixteenth century. (Artwork by F. Cannan-Braniff)

---

9 It is worth mentioning that, in Ireland, the surnames Welsh and Walsh are taken to mean descent from a Welsh person (quite possibly a Welsh soldier) – MacLysaght, *Surnames*, p.296; MacLysaght, *Irish Families*, p.155.
10 Quoted in Cannan, 'Hags of Hell,' p.15.
11 Guillaume le Clerc, *Fergus of Galloway*, trans. and ed. D. D. R. Owen (Edinburgh: John Donald, 2018), p.18.

THE GAELIC WORLD AT WAR: SOLDIERS & SOLDIERING IN IRELAND 1366-1547

Defying the so-called 'military revolution,' the last of the galloglass readies himself for action in the early seventeenth century. (drawing by F. Cannan-Braniff)

Military Accommodation

A horseman might be a gentleman living in some style in his own tower-house. But if he was a mercenary roving the country for employment or a younger son serving a chief as a mounted guard, he may well find himself allotted some rather basic accommodation by the marshal, as he moved with the chief from village to village and manor to manor.

In Ireland, it was common for soldiers to be billeted in the homes of the local community, which for the most part meant bedding down in huts and cabins, often the single-storey, windowless domed structures called 'coupled houses.'[12] Thackeray is spot on when he describes in his novel *Barry Lyndon* (first pub. 1844) Elizabethan English soldiers 'quartered with

---

12 S. Brindle, *Architecture in Britain and Ireland 1530–1830* (London: Yale University Press, 2023), p.118 on.

MARCSHLUA: THE 'KNIGHTS' OF A GAELIC ARMY

Barry's own gallowglasses, man by man in the cottages round about,'[13] after which fights break out and murders follow. However, Gaelic soldiers could live like this for free, eating and drinking their way through every available refreshment. A story, written down in the mid-seventeenth century, tells of a west Munster kern who had never seen an inn before and had no idea when he landed in England that he would have to pay for the food and drink he consumed, causing him to get beaten up...[14]

All the same, perceptions of Irish housing go wrong when historians forget that many of the poor in medieval England lived in housing that was just as dark, cramped and rickety. It is claimed, for instance, that the medieval village of Conisborough in Yorkshire was completely blown away in a gale, while in the church of St Benet, Cambridge, there survives a very old crook which, it is said, was wielded by a single man to pull down cottages that were on fire.[15]

Whether English or Irish, people appear to have done their best to make themselves look neat, tidy and respectable – but we are talking about the level of cleanliness one can achieve from washing in rivers, buckets and wells, and where many items of clothes were rarely, if ever, washed.[16] Living in cabins and bedding down on castle floors would have left even the most well-heeled horseman looking by our standards very rough, and it is hard to dismiss the accusation made by John Bale, Protestant Bishop of Ossory who was born in Suffolk in 1495, that come harvest time in rural Ireland gangs of horsemen, grooms, galloglass, kern and 'other brechlesse souldiers' would descend on villages, taking whatever they wanted, leaving behind nothing but penury, lechery and lice.[17]

---

13 W. M. Thackeray (A. Sanders, ed.), *The Memoirs of Barry Lyndon, Esq.* (Oxford: Oxford World's Classics, 1999), pp.3–4 & 138.
14 Simms, *Gaelic Ulster*, p.484.
15 R. J. Brown, *The English Country Cottage* (London: Robert Hale, 1979), p.21.
16 Thomas Sackville was Elizabeth I's Lord Treasurer and had 220 retainers on his daily roll at his home of Knole in Kent, but Knole appears to have had only a single wash basin and ewer! G. E. Fussell & K. R. Fussell, *The English Countrywoman: Her Life in Farmhouse and Field from Tudor Times to the Victorian Age* (London: Bloomsbury Books, 1985), p.27.
17 Hore & Graves, *Social State*, p.85.

8

Marshals & Constables: European Trends in Ireland

Constable, from the Latin *comes stabuli*, 'count officer of the stable'
Marshal, from an old Germanic term for 'horse servant'

The later Middle Ages in Ireland witnessed a major change in the way military command was regarded. Authority shifted from being a matter only of birthright, to an authority derived from holding an official position. In reality, commanders remained people of high birth, but they would now exercise their authority as holders of office.

This change was occurring across Europe. The appointment in the 1300s of Bertrand du Guesclin as 'Constable' (*Connétable*) of France is a key instance of this change, as is the appointment of William Wallace as 'Guardian' of his nation. The positions of constable and marshal had long existed in England, Scotland and France. But these titles appear to have acquired greater prominence and a wider range of responsibilities during the fierce wars involving England, France and Scotland in the late 1200s, 1300s and 1400s. These wars highlighted the need (especially in France and Scotland) for competent generals and trustworthy fighting viceroys who would keep on fighting even if the monarch was dead or incapable.

Charles Oman felt the Irish of Elizabeth I's time were 'absolutely unchanged' from their twelfth century ancestors, being as 'barbarous' as they had always been.[1] Yet the Irish landed classes participated enthusiastically in these trends, arranging their forces around two senior grades of officer: the constable and the marshal. Neither of the words 'constable' or 'marshal' are Gaelic in origin, but both became an important part of the language of command in Ireland in their Gaelicised forms, *marasgál* and *constábla*.[2]

---

1 Oman, *History*, vol. 1, p.411.
2 'Constable' and 'marshal' in *OED* and I. H. Evans, *Brewer's Dictionary of Phrase*

MARSHALS & CONSTABLES: EUROPEAN TRENDS IN IRELAND

From the 14th century there were Mac Domhnaill constables of galloglass in the army of Ó Neill (from at least the 1360s), and Ó Gallchobhair 'marshals of the hosts' and (from *c.* 1380) Mac Suibhne constables of galloglass in the army of Ó Domhnaill.³

Etymologically, the words constable and marshal both indicate responsibility for horses and cavalry, no doubt because of the social prestige cavalry had (sometimes still have) over infantry. In other words, within the new adoption of these titles was the old assumption that command of cavalry entailed command over all types of soldier. Irish annalists clearly knew the up-to-date military nomenclature, the *Annals of Inisfallen*

Irish horseman, 1640s. The Middle Ages is over and this Irish horseman rides to an uncertain future. This Irish horseman comes from a family that have done reasonably well out of the plantation land settlements; he could be from an old Gaelic family, an 'Old English' Anglo-Irish family, or one of the Scottish galloglass families. But his family's best days are long gone, as is his Gaelic attire. His clothing and equipment are no different to that of a cuirassier officer from anywhere in Europe. Only the squally landscape reminds us that he is in Ireland.
(Artwork by F. Cannan-Braniff)

---

    and Fable (London: Cassell, 1981, revd edn); 'consátbla' and 'marasgál' in the glossary of Simms, *Kings to Warlords*.

3 Simms, 'Images of the Galloglass', in Duffy, *World of the Galloglass*; p. 109; Nicholls, *Gaelic and Gaelicised Ireland*, p. 102.

recording that in 1309, 'Aed, son of Cathal, was treacherously slain by Mac Uigilin …. his own constable [*connsapla*].'[4] This may well have begun as a mimicking of the titles used by English knights. The twelfth century knight Hugh de Lacey was, for example, called by the *Annals of the Four Masters* 'Constable of the King of England [*Constapla righ Saxan*] in Dublin and East Meath.'[5] The difference is that in Ireland these titles were awarded by individual chiefs and lords, since there was no central national authority to do so. Some may see this as reflecting the fragmented, disunited nature of Ireland, but we might equally regard it as springing from the enduringly powerful belief among Irish chiefs that they were not lords but rulers of sovereign nations (and who is to say they were wrong?).

The Ó Gallchobhair Marshals

Probably because historians think galloglass were the only reliable soldiers in Ireland, the Ó Gallchobhair family, who held the post of Ó Domhnaill's *marasgál*, are now all but forgotten. The Ó Gallchobhair dynasty (whose name seems to mean 'foreign help') claimed to be the most senior of Ó Domhnaill's household families, the head of the Ó Gallchobhair family holding the post of *marasgál* of Ó Domhnaill's army from the fourteenth century, passing the title on a hereditary basis throughout the fifteenth and sixteenth centuries. With lands in Raphoe and Tirhugh, the senior branch of the family had a castle on an island called Inis Saimhéir (now Fish Island) at the mouth of the river Erne.[6] As well as soldiers, the family produced a remarkable number of senior churchmen: this was a powerful family involved in politics, war and the faith at a high level.

It was not only the Ó Domhnaills who had marshals. Fitzmaurice of Kerry was hereditary marshal to the Earls of Desmond, and it was stated in 1565 that 'Sir Owen O'Sullivan and his heirs' were 'one of the marshalls' of MacCarthy Mór.[7] Nor was it only the greatest dynasties who had marshals. The relatively minor Anglo-Irish family of Sutton gave the title of marshal and a castle called 'Old Court' to a junior kinsman,[8] and so even small living history groups portraying Ireland should consider appointing someone to that office. The Mac Domhnaill galloglass who entered Crown service are also described as having their own 'Marshal,' who, in 1557, was a man of 60 'yeres & upwarde' named 'Shane Burge'(Burgh?),[9] although they do not appear to have had particularly large forces. Marshals would have really

---

4   AI 1309.4.
5   AFM M1178.8.
6   Gillespie, 'Gaelic Families of Donegal,' in Nolan, Ronayne & Dunlevy, *Donegal*, pp.809–810; MacLysaght, *Irish Families*, p.91; MacLysaght, *Surnames*, p.117; McGettigan, *Red Hugh O'Donnell*, p.223.
7   Quoted in Hore, 'Life in Old Ireland,' p.273.
8   Hore, 'Life in Old Ireland,' p.273.
9   Hore, 'Rental Book of Gerald Fitzgerald,' p.276.

proved their worth during the *gairm shluaigh*, when they would have been kept busy imposing some sort of order on the assembled retinues of minor gentry, serving men and cattle-herders.

Seniority & Overlap

But who was the senior man, marshal or constable? According to Pisan the 'duc of batayles …. whome we calle now in fraunce Conestable' is the more senior; below the constable, she says, should be 'two marchallis' if we are 'folowyng thusage of fraunce.'[10] If the Ó Domhnaill followed the same protocol as France, then the Fanad Mac Suibhne constables would have been senior to the marshals, and probably second only to Ó Domhnaill himself. A clue that this was their protocol is that the Mac Suibhne of Fanad, the most senior of all Mac Suibhne lines, was permitted to sit at chief Ó Domhnaill's right hand side at feasts, 'whenever Mac Suibhne would visit.'[11] The right-side traditionally holding precedence over the left, all in attendance would thus see that Mac Suibhne Fanad was the chief's 'right-hand man.'

Irish use of the titles 'constable' and 'marshal' resembled French and English practice in two further ways. First is that, in Ireland as elsewhere, the two titles were not used precisely or consistently, and there was overlap between the roles of marshal and constable. Powerful chiefs (MacCarthy Mór, for instance) had multiple constables and marshals, with one of the constables and one of the marshals probably outranking the rest. The second similarity is that duties of Irish marshals and constables appear broadly the same as their English, French and other counterparts elsewhere. The duties of a marshal usually concerned discipline, billeting,[12] the arranging of soldiers into units and moving units into their correct position on the battlefield. Martin Martin speaks of the marshals in Hebridean lairds' retinues being experts in local family trees who would allot a seat to each person at banquet according to their status.[13] Such matters of precedence no doubt influenced the positioning of family units in musters, parades and on the battlefield. As late as the 1745–1746 rebellion, the MacDonalds and Murrays argued over who had the right to be positioned on the right-hand of the army.[14]

The constable, meanwhile, was generally considered to be the sovereign's viceroy or regional governor, though they would also be involved with overseeing disciplinary matters, and the arraying and inspecting of troops and equipment. From what we know, this was the case in Ireland, France and England. At times, a constable meant the governor of a single castle, or the

---

10   Pisan, *Book of Fayttes*, p.21.
11   *Leabhar Chlainne Suibhne*, p.43.
12   Simms, *Kings to Warlords*, p.95.
13   Martin, *Description*, p.81.
14   K. Tomasson & F. Buist, *Battles of the '45* (London: Pan, 1974), pp.46–47 & 161.

THE GAELIC WORLD AT WAR: SOLDIERS & SOLDIERING IN IRELAND 1366–1547

leader of a single band of galloglass, meaning that, though their jurisdiction was smaller, they were nevertheless their prince's representative.

In reality, the two titles were probably sometimes little more than a formal recognition that a person had been admitted to the leader's inner circle, and that they had pledged to play a leading role in defence and the sourcing and organising of soldiers. Whether by accident or design, the blurred lines of command and overlapping responsibilities between constable and marshal no doubt helped prevent any one retainer becoming too powerful. There was always the possibility of rivalry and rebellion from major vassal families such as that of Mac Suibhne and Ó Gallchobhair.[15] Bestowing prestigious titles was a way of flattering the egos of not quite your enemies, but certainly your potential rivals. As with all medieval royal courts, there was intrigue and jostling for position. But there must also have been a realisation among Irish chiefs that command and control could only happen if they had dependable deputies to hand whose loyalty and duties had been officially codified.

Irish soldiers, perhaps a foraging party returning to camp, in Henry VIII's army at the siege of Boulogne in 1544. The image (510 mm x 1610 mm) is an engraving by James Basire the elder (1730-1802), published 1788. The engraving is based on Tudor murals at Cowdray House, Sussex; the murals and most of the house were destroyed in a fire in 1793. The Irish soldiers appear to be barelegged but wearing shoes. Several appear to wear helmets while some are wearing hats. (© Royal Academy of Arts, London, Object No. 17/1278)

Given the prestige and authority of titles like marshal and constable, what if, in another reality, a Mac Suibhne, a Ó Gallchobhair or even a Keating had bypassed the magnates and assumed national command? Might they have been able to transform regional, factional uprisings into a Hussite-style war of national liberation? Could they have become an Irish William Wallace, Joan of Arc or Jan Žižka? Might then the peasant forces of *ceithearnaigh* and *gairm shluaigh* have been galvanised into a fearsome rural militia like that of Switzerland, stiffened by the heavy assault tactics of the *gallóglaigh*?

---

15   Relations between two branches of the Ó Gallchobhair family were tense, and similarly between some of the Ó Gallchobhair family and their Ó Domhnaill chiefs. In 1546 Domhnall Ó Domhnaill was murdered by one of the Ó Gallchobhair sept, Eoghan mac Éamainn, at Inis Saimhéir: Gillespie, 'Gaelic Families,' in Nolan, Ronayne & Dunlevy, *Donegal*, p.811; A. Cathcart, 'James V, King of Scotland – and Ireland?', in Duffy, *World of the Galloglass*, p.136, n. 53.

9

The Collapse of the Gaelic Recovery

> I have had much satisfaction among the Mac Swinies, a glorious race worthy of their magnanimous ancestors, and I am sorry to have to announce to you that the present chief of the Mac Swinies Doe has been obliged to exchange the battle axe and sword for the Budget and the soldering iron.
>
> Letter from John O'Donovan to the historian Eugene O'Curry, 14 September 1835

But it was not to be. In Donegal in the summer of 1835 John O'Donovan met two MacSweeneys who were considered to be the heirs to Fanad and Doe. Both were living in very modest circumstances, O'Donovan writing that the MacSweeney Doe he met rode a donkey instead of a 'richly caparisoned steed,' following the life of a traveller and metalworker.[1] 'Tinker' has become an insult, but it originally meant a skilled metalworker and metal-goods repairer, and from Rathmullan on 30 August 1835, O'Donovan wrote with no disrespect, '…the heir of Fanaid is said to be a tinker who strolls through the country and sometimes comes to visit his castle at Rathmullan and to give orders to Knoxe's man to take particular care of it!'[2]

In or around 1618, the MacSweeneys had lost Rathmullan to Andrew Knox (or Knoxe), Protestant Bishop of Raphoe.[3] MacSweeneys, 'called Mac Swynes here' says O'Donovan, knew their family history, though.[4]

---

1   O'Donovan letter of 14th September 1835: RIA 14/C/11/15, p.2.
2   O'Donovan letter of 30th August 1835: RIA 14/C/11/9, pp.2–3.
3   O'Donovan letter of 30th August 1835: RIA 14/C/11/9, p.2; Archdall, *Monasticon*, vol. 1, p.213.
4   O'Donovan letter of 30th August 1835: RIA 14/C/11/9, p.2.

O'Donovan recalled he had the 'honor of shaking hands' with the heir to Doe and 'of saluting him (with my hat off)'. O'Donovan addressed 'the present chief of the Mac Swinnies Doe' as 'commander-in-chief of the forces of O'Donnell, firebrand glowing inextinguishable, and defender of the gap of danger,' to which Doe responded 'with serious satisfaction.'[5] Their status had changed but many of the old families remained living in their ancestral districts. A century later, in 1938, schoolchildren participating in a folklore project were told by a farmer aged 'about 76' that Moross or 'McSweeney's Castle' lay on 'Pat Sweeney's farm by the Mulroy.'[6]

The odds Irish warriors faced were enormous. By the late Middle Ages, England had one of the best armies in the known world, strong seafaring abilities, a thriving economy and (despite occasional civil wars) central government. Ireland, on the other hand, was a patchwork of lordships and, ultimately, factionalism proved far more damaging to the effectiveness of Irish armies than the armour they wore, the weapons they used or the fighting techniques they mastered. The belief that military strength and expertise were best provided by foreigners (Scots, English and Welsh mercenaries, Spaniards and also Anglo-Irish outlaws) was also not always beneficial in the long term.

England also attempted to conquer Scotland; this time England failed. But Scotland had had a century longer than Ireland to grow and develop before experiencing English invasion. Moreover, Edward I was so unpleasant that he hammered the Scots into one nation, whereas the English invasion of Ireland in the late 1100s was far less clear cut. Given the political and economic disadvantages facing Gaelic Irish armies, it is extraordinary they fought so well.

A level-headed galloglass, kern or horseman getting ready for war with the English would have known they were the underdogs and that they would need to train, plan and fight all the harder to stand a chance of winning. It was always going to be an uphill struggle. But it was not a one-sided struggle. It was not a war between two different worlds. Defeat was not inevitable.

Historians call Irish warriors disorganised, bloodthirsty and backward. But they were not always badly equipped. They were not always poorly trained. They were not unaware of the importance of logistics. They were not in bad physical shape (far from it). They were not unaware of military theory. They were not unaware of new trends in military thinking. They were not poorly led. They were not without resolve or resourcefulness. They were better than that.

---

5   O'Donovan letter of 14th September 1835: RIA 14/C/11/15, p.2.
6   Dúchas.ie: Schools' Collection, volume 1089, p.212.

Colour Plate Commentaries

Plate A. Ó Gallchobhair horseman, late 1300s.

This high-status cavalry man from the Ó Gallchobhair or O'Gallagher family – one of Donegal's premier dynasties – has heard Richard II is in Ireland with a large and powerful force, and has thus readied himself for action. He wears a bascinet with mail aventail, mail shirt and quilted tunic to keep out weaponry, and a wool cloak and hood to keep out the elements. His legs and feet, however, are bare – not a sign of poverty but an ostentatious show of hardiness. Irish shields have not been properly studied, but from the available evidence they appear to have been similar to the round, leather-covered wooden 'targes' used in Scotland.

Plate B. Galloglass standard bearer in the service of the Butlers of Ormond, early 1400s.

The aural spookiness of the word *galloglass* has caught the imagination of those in the creative arts. Shakespeare mentions galloglass in *Macbeth* and *Henry VI Part 2*, just as *Gallowglass* was the title of a creepy thriller about power by Barbara Vine (1990), and there has been a German metal band called *Galloglass*, and a 2019 fantasy novel of the same name by Scarlett Thomas.

The very etymology of 'galloglass' reveals something of the salient characteristics of this distinctive class of warrior. The Irish origin for 'galloglass' is *gallóglach* (singular), or *gallóglaigh* (plural). The gender of the term happens to be masculine – and, indeed, there are no recorded female galloglass, though there were noblewomen who hired galloglass and had them in their retinues. The word is formed from two Irish words: *gall* ('foreign', 'stranger') and *óglach* ('youth', 'servant', 'vassal', 'retainer'). *Óglach* can be traced back to two Old Irish words: *oc* ('young') and the suffix *ach* which is used in Irish to make a connection between a person or thing and another quality – for instance if we add *ach* to *Sasana* ('England') we get *Sasanach* ('English'). Soldiers, members of sports teams and servants have often been addressed as 'boys' or 'lads', creating a clubby atmosphere of male heartiness (and also because soldiers and sportspeople are often very young), giving the *óglach* component of *gallóglach* connotations of military or clan/feudal service.[1]

As one word, *gallóglach* therefore translates literally as 'young foreign warrior' or 'young foreign retainer'. Nevertheless, we need to be careful with the 'foreign' element in *gallóglach*. We could understand this to mean that the galloglass were foreigners in Ireland. But it is more likely that *gall* is a reference not to foreignness but to the *Innse Gall*, the Scottish Gaelic name for the Hebrides, from where so many of the original galloglass hailed. If so, the word *gallóglach* would have signified to the Irish of the time a 'Hebridean warrior' or 'Hebridean retainer'. This 'Hebridean retainer' bears the colours of the Earl of Ormond. Although some of his equipment is a little old fashioned, it is good quality and there is plenty of it.

Plate C. 'Rising out' husbandman, mid-1400s.

E. P. Thompson spoke of 'history from below' and this is an attempt at Gaelic military history from below. This Irish 'husbandman', or small-time farmer of sub-yeoman status, has armed himself as best he can in response to his chief's call to arms. We are in speculative, unexplored territory here, but the aim of the plate is to demonstrate that just because Irish peasant conscripts must often have been poor, they were not necessarily badly equipped.

For a start, ordinary people in the Middle Ages were most certainly not physically feeble or incapable of defending themselves. In 1513 raiders attacking Killybegs harbour were repulsed by a young member of the Mac Suibhne family and local shepherds and farmers helped, it was believed, by the 'miracles of God and St Catherine'. One very much hopes, too, that the story of Finlay na Plaide Baine, an ordinary clansman near Dunvegan in Scotland, is true. The story goes that Finlay sorted out a gang of *buannachan* (a chief's professional military) with his ash flail after they killed his best cow; he then tied the gang up, using only one rope to tie each man's neck, wrists and ankles together. It should be no surprise, then, that a 1517 decree in the Ormond lordship expected 'husbandmen' to 'rise in defence' of the area with 'the horsemen, Scots, footmen and all others.'

This husbandman's main weapon is a flail (which, being a rural man, he probably knows how to use since he may well use the farm-tool version in peacetime). As further weaponry, he has a short knife, a sickle and a home-made javelin. His thick hood and tunic will give some protection against slashing blades, and he has made himself a leather-covered shield and a

---

1 Once the word entered the English language, it became common to spell the word 'gallowglass', and some modern writers prefer this spelling. The 'w' spelling looks, to me, rather clumsy, and so does the plural 'gallowglasses' – but this is personal choice and not a matter of correct and incorrect.

leather cap, and he holds a very damaged, very old (1300s) bascinet which he has either found, been lent from a castle armoury or bought cheap from a galloglass.

Plate D. Galloglass fighting for the Earl of Desmond, battle of Piltown, 1462.

One of the great myths of Gaelic history is that nothing changed. This plate illustrates that Gaelic armies did change and evolve. This Mac Síthigh or MacSheehy galloglass is not a quixotic Viking-style warrior living in the past, but a well-equipped Wars of the Roses-era soldier. Students of Talhoffer will recognise the galloglass' stance, which has been modelled on Talhoffer's instructional illustrations for pole-axe combat. Fought between the Fitzgeralds of Desmond and the Butlers of Ormond, the battle of Piltown (Co. Kilkenny) was a tough engagement by any standards, demonstrating that Irish forces had staying power (despite what modern historians have claimed).

Plate E. Kern at the battle of Stoke, 1487.

Piecing together what happened at Stoke is not easy. What we know is that a large number of Irish soldiers, led by Thomas Fitzgerald, fought there for Lambert Simnel. Historians have assumed they were all kern and that Simnel's defeat at Stoke was at least partly their fault, since, supposedly, they wore no armour, were badly equipped and were reckless maniacs who knew nothing of modern war. Most of these assumptions are unsupported by evidence, and we are under no compulsion to accept any of the above as true.

Certainly, the kern was a light infantryman but it is impossible to believe that they would have arrived at Stoke without any regard for bodily protection. This plate is a conjectural response to Stanihurst's claim that kern did not wear 'heavy armour', and to the fact that Ireland was a relatively poor nation, and getting supplies was not easy. And so this kern wears light-weight armour, and old, affordable kit – but it will do the job. Over his saffron-dyed shirt, he wears a sleeveless padded jerkin, and his head is protected by an arming cap and a helmet that is more than a century old; but, again, it still works. He carries a small shield, javelins and sword, and has a long Irish knife. 16th-century images show Irish warriors with a single gauntlet on the left hand, and here we hypothesise it would be easy enough to make an iron gauntlet for the right hand.

Plate F. Runner in the Earl of Kildare's service, late 15th century

This combative little character is a 'runner' in the employ of the Fitzgeralds of Kildare. Already weapons-trained (he may well be the son of a kern or galloglass), his attire is a mix of Irish (his cloak, long knife and javelin) and English and overseas influences (his jacket, shoes and battered kettle hat) as his employers, the Fitzgeralds, are the leading family in and around the so-called 'Pale', or area of English authority in Ireland.

Stanihurst refers to 'runners' in Irish armies, by which he may well mean messengers and errand-boys. The role of children in Irish armies has been overlooked, even though there were children in a number of what we can call servant-combatant roles – that is, servants and camp followers who might sometimes join in with the fighting. In the 1500s there were many boy runners in the Kildare household, and Dymmok tells us the 'horsboyes' who served as grooms in Irish armies would join in with the fighting, hurling javelins; in Dymmok's opinion they were 'skumme'. Given they were entrusted with the vital job of looking after the horses, one wonders if some of this 'scum' were actually pages, squire-like apprentice warriors, and not just street urcheons or artful dodger types (or 'outcaste of the cuntrye' as Dymmok puts it).

Plate G. 'Redshank' Highland mercenary in Ireland, *c.* 1500

There is no evidence to support the assertion, often made by historians, that only wealthy Highlanders wore armour. In fact, it is possible to argue that the typical Highland soldier was probably better equipped than the average Lowland recruit, and indeed than many English soldiers. Historians deem Highland battle-dress primitive and basic, but practical and comfortable is a more accurate assessment. Highlanders clearly had first-class weapons skills as well as practical and comfortable clothing and armour, and this man is a proficient archer as well as swordsman. He holds his bow while a ghillie, waiting behind him, carries a two-handed sword for him. We have taken the liberty of representing his helmet as painted with religious imagery, since we suggest that the painting of armour was probably fairly widespread. The painted imagery will protect the helmet from rust and, the Highlander hopes, protect the wearer's body and soul in battle.

Plate H. Edmund Purcell, captain of kern, serving with Henry VIII in France, 1544-45.

Anyone who believes that Irish armies were incapable of change should compare this plate with plate A. The change is obvious. Other than his tomb, we have no visual record for Purcell, and so we have imagined him as a light infantry officer with a blending of Irish and English traditions. Here we catch Purcell in a moment of private devotion, wrapped in his thick Irish cloak, an essential campaign item. Kern were often regarded as swordsmen and so we have given Purcell both a fine sword and a buckler, based on a surviving example from near Wrexham of about 1500 and now in the Metropolitan Museum, New York. The Metropolitan Museum buckler, which is covered in pigskin, bears more than a passing resemblance to Scottish targes, and presumably Irish ones – so the reader is free to interpret the buckler shown here as either something Purcell acquired from Wales, or as a shield resembling those used by Irish warriors.

Purcell's German helmet, sword and clothes are fairly new and fashionable. His German body armour is sound in quality but old, having probably been acquired by the previous generation and reused by Edmund. In part this is because provincial Ireland is off the beaten track for European arms-dealers, but partly also because people (of many nations) did use old armour – not necessarily always out of poverty, given that family heirlooms have style and class and give one a sense of pride and connection with the past.

Plate I.

One of Dürer's Irish warriors drawn by an unknown female artist for the Irish antiquary William Hugh Patterson (1835-1918) (Royal Irish Academy).

Plate J.

Christ carrying the Cross from the 16th-century history of the Burke family, the 'Book of the De Burgos'. Christ is surrounded by four Roman soldiers and several other figures – all of whom are clearly modelled on Irishmen and galloglass (The Board of Trinity College Dublin).

Plate K.

Supposedly made from life, the date of this image of Irishmen is uncertain but it probably dates from the mid to late 16th century. (© Ashmolean Museum, University of Oxford).

Plate L.

By any standard, Art Mór Mac Murchadha Caomhánach was a gifted commander. Reviving the title of king of Leinster, Art fought two campaigns against Richard II and remained until his death in 1416/17 master of his lands. Here we see Art, decorated lance raised above his head, riding down from the hills to negotiate with the Earl of Gloucester. Behind Art are two hooded Irish horsemen. The image, an illustration from Jean Creton's account of Richard II's downfall, was made while Art was still alive. Creton was in Ireland with Richard II in 1399 and it is possible this depiction of Art is an accurate portrait based on memories of the campaign. Modern interpretations of this image show King Art wearing early medieval-style armour. In fact, his equipment is not that antique; he just has less of it than the English men-at-arms who watch him. Art wears a bascinet with what appears to be gilded decoration, mail shirt and a sharply-pointed scabbard can be seen – perhaps for a thrusting sword or maybe for an Irish scian dagger (© The Board of the British Library).

Plate M.

Horseman in the 16th-century 'Book of the De Burgos', in fairly heavy armour but no stirrups, and with lance held over arm rather than couched. (The Board of Trinity College Dublin).

Plate N.

Like a Gaelic Irish horseman, he is armed for mobile, hit-and-run warfare. Unlike a Gaelic horseman, he has stirrups. His stocky horse's harness (his horse is more finely harnessed than he is), and the lowest of the three hand-and-a-half swords shown here, are taken from a *c.* 1500 wall painting of St. George in St. Gregory's church, Norwich. The 'pavise' shield bears one version of the Preston arms. The effigy (to the right of the horseman) has been identified as William Preston (d. 1532); William fought on the winning side at Knockdoe as a commander of archers. All the illustration's other items have an English provenance. At the top of the picture is a 15th-century spur, and medieval pottery oil lamp and horseshoe: all three items were found in Pevensey Castle (and are now in Michelham Priory). The spearhead (neck broken in two) was probably found in Surrey. The mid-15th century Clare reliquary cross (British Museum) hangs below the spearhead; made of gold, pearls and originally enamelled, it was found on the site of Clare Castle, Norfolk, in 1866. The top two swords are (left) the civic sword of Dublin (probably supplied to Dublin's mayor from the personal arsenal of Henry IV), and (right) an early 15th-century hand-and-a-half sword which may be English (now in the Royal Armouries).

COLOUR PLATE COMMENTARIES

Plate O.

Spur found at Clontarf, Co. Dublin. Probably made by an Irish craftsperson, it likely dates from late Middle Ages but could be as late as 17th century (© National Museum of Ireland).

Plate P.

Jacket found as part of a suit of clothes at Kilcommon, Co. Tipperary. Of a style long established in Ireland, this example is probably late 16th or early 17th century. The jacket is made of coarse woven wool and buttons at the front and cuffs. There is a slash opening at each shoulder for fashionable effect (© National Museum of Ireland).

Plate Q.

Galloglass at prayer, around 1600, at the chapel of Gartan in Donegal, birthplace of St. Colum Cille; painted by Fergus Cannan-Braniff. The ruins of the chapel, known to have been once thatched, still stand. We have attempted here a reconstruction of the last era of galloglass, based on an interpretation of John Thomas' picture-map of the battle of Erne Fords. We have given the galloglass a ceramic hand grenade (on the ground by his knee) based on an example now in the Ulster Museum which came from a Spanish ship, Trinidad Valencera; the ship had participated in the 1588 Armada campaign and was wrecked in Kinnagoe Bay, Donegal.

Plate R.

A 'corrected' version of Dürer famous depiction of Irish warriors, made from scratch as an etching with watercolour by Russell Moore in 2025. This, the author and Moore suggest, is what Dürer would have drawn if he had really seen Irishmen with his own eyes. Changes include long Irish knives, galloglass-type axes instead of glaives, reducing the size of the two-handed sword, and giving the two men on the right Irish jackets rather than the loose, unmilitary late medieval coat seen in Dürer's original (a style of jacket Dürer also includes in his portrait of his 70-year-old father in the National Gallery, London).

Bibliography

Primary Sources, Manuscripts

Lambeth Palace Library: Carew Mss 601 f.35; 621 ff.106–111; 625 f.1; 635 ff.92a, 146r and 163V

National Archives (London): SP 63/51/42

National Library of Ireland: Book of Funeral Entries, volume 3 (1604–1622)

Royal Irish Academy: papers relating to John O'Donovan and the Ordnance Survey (Mss 14/B/7, 14/C/11/15 and 14/C/11/9); letter with accompanying drawing from William Hugh Patterson to James Graves (Ms 24 O 39/JG/11a); and a page of Gaelic poetry about MacSweeney Fanad: Ms 475 (24/P/25), f.76v

Trinity College Dublin: the 'Book of the de Burgos' (IE TCD MS 1440).

Objects and associated files in museums including Ashmolean Museum, Dublin Castle, Hunterian Museum, National Museum of Ireland, Somerset Museum, Tate Britain, Ulster Museum

Primary Sources, Published

State Papers, Vol. II: King Henry the Eighth, Part 3 (London: HMSO, 1834)

Archdall, Mervyn, *Monasticon Hibernicum*, volume 1 (Dublin: W.B. Kelly, 1873)

Barry, Great, *A Discourse of Military Discipline* (Brussels: Widow of John Mommart, 1634)

Camden, William, *Annales*, volume 1 (London: William Stansbury & Simon Waterson, 1615)

Camden, William, (E. Gibson, trans. & ed.), *Britannia*, volume 2 (London: W. Bowyer etc., 1772)

Carlyle, Alexander (J. Kinsley, ed.), *Anecdotes and Characters of the Times* (London: Oxford University Press, 1973)

Caxton, William, *The Description of Britain*, ed. M. Collins (London: Guild, 1988)

Derricke, John (F. J. Sypher ed.) *The Image of Irelande: With a Discouerie of Woodkarne*, (Delmar: Scholars' Facsimiles & Reprints, 1998)

Dymmok, John, *A Treatice of Ireland* (Dublin: Irish Archaeological Society, 1842)

Edgeworth, Maria (G. Watson, ed.) *Castle Rackrent* (Oxford: Oxford World's Classics, 2008)

Froissart, Jean, (G. Brereton, trans. & ed.) *Chronicles* (London: Penguin, 1978)

Gainsford, Thomas, *The Glory of England* (London, E. Griffin, 1620, 2nd edn)

Gerald of Wales (J. J. O'Meara, trans.) *The History and Topography of Ireland* (London: Penguin, 1982)

Guillaume le Clerc (D. D. R. Owen, trans. and ed.) *Fergus of Galloway* (Edinburgh: John Donald, 2018)

Haslewood, J, (ed.) *Mirror for Magistrates*, volume 2 (London: Lackington, Allen & Co., 1815)

Hogan, E. (ed.), *The Description of Ireland, and the State Thereof as it is at This Present in Anno 1598* (Dublin & London: M.H. Gill & Bernard Quaritch, 1878)

Holinshed, Raphael, *Chronicles*, volume 2 (London: J. Harrison, 1587, 2nd edn)

Hooker, John (J. Maclean ed.), *The Life and Times of Sir Peter Carew, Kt*, (London: Bell & Dandy, 1857)

Lindsay of Pitscottie, Robert (ed. Æ. J. G Mackay), *The Historie and Cronicles of Scotland* volume 1 (Edinburgh: Scottish Text Society, 1899)

Logan, James & McIan, R. R., *The Clans of the Scottish Highlands* (London: Chancellor Press 1985)

Mackenzie, John (W. D. Killen ed.), *Memorials of the Siege of Derry* (Belfast: C. Aitchison, 1861)

Martin, Martin, *A Description of the Western Isles of Scotland* (London: Andrew Bell, 1703. Edinburgh: Birlinn, 2018 reprint)

Meyrick, Samuel Rush (ed.), *Heraldic Visitations of Wales and Part of the Marches*, volume 2 (Llandovery: William Rees, 1846)

Mills J. & McEnery, M. J. (eds), *Calendar of the Gormanston Register, From the Original in the Possession of the Right Honourable the Viscount of Gormanston*, (Dublin: Dublin University Press, 1916)

M'Laughlan, T. (trans. and ed.), *The Dean of Lismore's Book* (Edinburgh: Edmonston & Douglas, 1862)

More, Thomas, (P. Turner trans. and ed.), *Utopia*, trans. and ed. P. Turner (London: Penguin, 2003)

O'Donnell, Manus (B. Lacey ed.), *The Life of Colum Cille* (Dublin: Four Courts Press, 1994).

O'Donovan J. (trans. and ed.) *Annals of the Kingdom of Ireland, by the Four Masters*, volume 4 (Dublin, 1856, 2nd edn)

Pennant, Thomas, *A Tour in Scotland 1769* (Chester: John Monk, 1771. Edinburgh: Birlinn, 2019 reprint)

Piccope, G. J. (ed.), *Lancashire and Cheshire Wills and Inventories from the Ecclesiastical Court, Chester* (Manchester: The Chetham Society, 1861), 3rd portion

Pisan, Christine de (William Caxton trans. A. T. P. Byles ed.), *The Book of Fayttes of Armes and of Chyvalrye* (Oxford: Early English Text Society & Kraus Reprint Co., 1971)

Renatus, Flavius Vegetius (J. Clarke trans.), *De Re Militari* (Milton Keynes: Leonaur, 2012)

Rich, Barnabe, *A New Description of Ireland* (London, Thomas Adams, 1610)

Stanihurst, Richard (L. Miller & E. Power eds), *Holinshed's Irish Chronicle* (Dublin: Dolmen, 1979)

Stanihurst, Richard (J. Barry & H. Morgan trans. and ed.), *Great Deeds in Ireland* (Togher: Cork University Press, 2015)

Stow, John (H. Morely ed.), *A Survey of London Written in the Year 1598* (Stroud: Sutton, 1999)

Talhoffer, Hans (M. Rector trans. & ed.), *Medieval Combat: A Fifteenth-Century Illustrated Manual of Swordfighting and Close-Quarter Combat* (London: Greenhill, 2000)

Walsh, P. (trans. & ed.), *Leabhar Chlainne Suibhne: An Account of the MacSweeney Families in Ireland* (Dublin: Dollard Printing House, 1920)

Ware, James, *The Antiquities and History of Ireland* (Dublin: A. Crook, 1705)

Published Books, Secondary

Allmand, C., *The De Re Militari of Vegetius: The Reception, Transmission and Legacy of a Roman Text in the Middle Ages* (Cambridge: Cambridge University Press, 2013)

Asbridge, T., *The Greatest Knight* (London: Simon & Schuster, 2015)

Bagwell, R., *Ireland Under the Tudors*, volume 3 (London: Longmans, Green & Co., 1890)

Bailey, M., *Dürer* (London: Phaidon, 1995)

Bartlett, C., *English Longbowman 1330–1515*, Warrior Series no.13 (Oxford: Osprey, 2020)

Bartlett, T. & Jeffrey, K. (eds.), *A Military History of Ireland* (Cambridge: Cambridge University Press, 1996)

Barr, N., *Flodden* (Stroud: Tempus, 2003)

Bradbury, J., *The Medieval Archer* (Woodbridge: Boydell Press, 1997)

Brindle, S., *Architecture in Britain and Ireland 1530–1830* (London: Yale University Press, 2023)

Brown, R. J., *The English Country Cottage* (London: Robert Hale, 1979)

Burke, B., *The General Armory of England, Scotland, Ireland, and Wales* (Ramsbury: Heraldry Today, 1989)

Campbell, M., *The English Yeoman Under Elizabeth and the Stuarts* (London: Merlin, 1983)

Cannan, F., *Scottish Arms and Armour* (Oxford: Shire, 2009)

Cannan, F., *Galloglass 1250–1600: Gaelic Mercenary Warrior*, Warrior Series no. 143 (Oxford: Osprey, 2010)

Chrimes, S. B., *Henry VII* (New Haven & London: Yale University Press, 1999)

Connolly, S. J. (ed.), *The Oxford Companion to Irish History* (Oxford: Oxford University Press, 2011, 2nd edn)

Curry, A. (ed.), *Agincourt 1415: Henry V, Sir Thomas Erpingham and the Triumph of the English Archers* (Stroud: Tempus, 2000)

Deevy, M. B., *Medieval Ring Brooches in Ireland* (Bray: Wordwell, 1998)

Duffy S. (ed.), *The World of the Galloglass: Kings, Warlords and Warriors in Ireland and Scotland, 1200–1600* (Dublin: Four Courts Press, 2007)

Duffy S. (ed.), *Robert the Bruce's Irish Wars: The Invasions of Ireland 1306–1329* (Stroud: Tempus, 2002)

Dunbar, J. T., *History of Highland Dress* (London: Batsford, 1978)

Dunlevy, M., *Dress in Ireland: A History* (Wilton: Doughcloyne, 1999)

Ellis, S. G., *Ireland in the Age of the Tudors 1447–1603: English Expansion and the End of Gaelic Rule* (Abingdon: Routledge, 2014)

Evans, I. H., *Brewer's Dictionary of Phrase and Fable* (London: Cassell, 1981, revd edn)

Fussell, G. E. & K. R., *The English Countrywoman: Her Life in Farmhouse and Field from Tudor Times to the Victorian Age* (London: Bloomsbury Books, 1985)

Gillingham, J., *The Wars of the Roses: Peace & Conflict in 15th Century England* (London: Phoenix Press, 2002)

Gregory, D., *History of the Western Highlands and Isles of Scotland from AD 1493 to AD 1625 with a Brief Introductory Sketch From AD 80 to AD 1493* (Vancouver: Eremitical Press, 2009)

Gresh, R., *The Skean: The Distinctive Fighting Knife of Gaelic Ireland 1500–1700* (Atglen, PA: Schiffer, 2023)

Harris, J. & Sidwell, K. (eds.), *Making Ireland Roman: Irish Neo-Latin Writers and the Republic of Letters* (Togher: Cork University Press, 2009)

Hayes-McCoy, G. A., *Irish Battles: A Military History of Ireland* (Belfast: Appletree Press, 1990)

Hayes-McCoy, G. A., *Scots Mercenary Forces in Ireland (1567–1603)* (Dublin: Edmund Burke, 1996)

Haythornthwaite, P., *The English Civil War 1642–1651: An Illustrated Military History* (Poole: Blandford Press, 1983)

Higgins, I. M., *Writing East: The 'Travels' of Sir John Mandeville* (Philadelphia: University of Pennsylvania Press, 1997)

Higgins, J., *Galway's Heritage in Stone*, Galway City Museum catalogue no. 1 (Galway: Galway City Museum, 2006)

Hore H. F. & J. Graves, J. (eds.), *The Social State of the Southern and Eastern Counties of Ireland in the 16th Century* (Dublin: Kilkenny and South East Ireland Archaeological Society, 1870)

Hunt, D., *A History of Preston* (Lancaster: Carnegie, revd edn 2002)

Hutchinson, R., *The Audacious Crimes of Colonel Blood* (London: Weidenfeld & Nicolson, 2016)

Laking, G. F., *A Record of European Armour and Arms Through Seven Centuries*, volume 5 (Milton Keynes: Benediction Classics, 2009)

BIBLIOGRAPHY

Lawrence, D. R., *The Complete Soldier: Military Books and Military Culture in Early Stuart England, 1603–1645* (Leiden: Brill, 2009)

MacAlpine N. & Mackenzie, J., *Gaelic-English and English-Gaelic Dictionary* (Glasgow: Gairm Publications, 1971)

MacGregor, R., *Memorials of the Bass Rock* (Edinburgh: James Gremmell, 1881)

Mackay, C., *The Auld Scots Dictionary* (Glasgow: Lang Syne, 2002)

McKenzie, C. J. & Murphy, E. M., *Life and Death in Medieval Gaelic Ireland: The Skeletons from Ballyhanna, Co. Donegal* (Dublin: Four Courts Press, 2018).

MacLennan, M., *A Pronouncing and Etymological Dictionary of the Gaelic Language* (Stornoway & Aberdeen: Acair & Aberdeen University Press, 1982)

MacLysaght, E., *Irish Families: Their Names, Arms & Origins* (Blackrock: Irish Academic Press, 1991, 4th edn)

MacLysaght, E., *The Surnames of Ireland* (Sallins: Irish Academic Press, 2023, 6th edn)

Mann, J., *European Arms and Armour* (London & Beccles: The Wallace Collection, 1962), volume 2: *Arms*

Marsden, J. *Galloglas: Hebridean and West Highland Mercenary Warrior Kindreds in Medieval Ireland* (East Linton: Tuckwell, 2015)

McGettigan, D., *Red Hugh O'Donnell and the Nine Years' War* (Dublin: Four Courts Press, 2005)

McGettigan, D., *Richard II and the Irish Kings* (Dublin: Four Courts Press, 2016)

O'Hart, J., *Irish Pedigrees*, volumes 1 & 2 (Dublin: James Duffy & Co., 1892, 5th edn)

Ó Mianáin P. (chief ed.), *Concise English-Irish Dictionary: Foclóir Béarla-Gaeilge* (Dublin: Foras na Gaeilge, 2021)

McNamee, C., *The Wars of the Bruces: Scotland, England and Ireland, 1306–1328* (Phantassie: Tuckwell, 1997)

Miller, D., *Irish Swordsmanship: Fencing and Duelling in Eighteenth Century Ireland* (New York: Hudson Society, 2017)

Morrill J. (ed.), *The Oxford Illustrated History of Tudor & Stuart Britain* (Oxford: Oxford University Press, 1996)

Nicholls, K., *Gaelic and Gaelicized Ireland* (Dublin: Lilliput Press, 2003, 2nd edn)

Nicolson, A. (A. Maclean ed.), *History of Skye* (Portree: Maclean Press, 1930, revd edn)

Nolan, W., Ronayne L. & Dunlevy, M. (eds.), *Donegal: History and Society* (Dublin: Geography Publications, 1995)

Oman, C., *History of the Art of War in the Middle Ages*, volume 1 (Oxford: Blackwell, 1885. Uckfield: Naval & Military Press reprint)

O'Neill, J., *The Nine Years' War, 1593–1603: O'Neill, Mountjoy and the Military Revolution* (Dublin: Four Courts Press, 2017)

Palmer, R. (ed.), *The Rambling Soldier* (Gloucester: Alan Sutton, 1985)

Pullein-Thompson, J., *Horses and Their Owners* (London: Nelson, 1970)

Richey, A. G. (R. R. Kane ed.), *A Short History of the Irish People* (Dublin: Hodges, Figgis and Co., 1887)

Roberts, K., *Soldiers of the English Civil War (1): Infantry*, Elite Series no. 25 (Oxford: Osprey, 1989)

Rowse, A. L. *The Expansion of Elizabethan England* (London: Macmillan, 1971)

Scott, B. G., *Early Irish Ironworking*, Ulster Museum Publication No. 266 (Belfast: Ulster Museum, 1998)

Simms, K., *From Kings to Warlords: The Changing Political Structure of Gaelic Ireland in the Later Middle Ages* (Woodbridge: Boydell Press, 1987)

Simms, K., *Gaelic Ulster in the Middle Ages: History, Culture and Society* (Dublin: Four Courts Press: 2020)

Thackeray, W. M. (A. Sanders ed.), *The Memoirs of Barry Lyndon, Esq.* (Oxford: Oxford World Classics, 1999)

Thomson, J. A. F., *The Transformation of Medieval England 1370–1529* (Harlow: Longman, 1995)

Tomasson, K. & Buist, F., *Battles of the '45* (London: Pan, 1974)

Tsui, B., *Why We Swim* (London: Penguin, 2020)

Tyerman, C., *How to Plan a Crusade: Reason and Religious War in the High Middle Ages* (London: Penguin, 2016)

Verbruggen, J. F. (S. Willard & R. W. Southern, trans.), *The Art of Warfare in Western Europe During the Middle Ages* (Woodbridge: Boydell, revd edn 1998)

Watson, A., *The Essential Gaelic-English English-Gaelic Dictionary* (Edinburgh: Birlinn, 2012)

Journals and Chapters

Borrowes, E. D., 'Tennekille Castle, Portarlington, and Glimpses of the MacDonnells' in *Ulster Journal of Archaeology*, 1st series, volume 2 (1854), pp.34–43

Bourke, C., 'A Medieval Helmet from Lough Henney, Co. Down' in *Lecale Miscellany*, no. 8 (1990), pp.5–7

Bourke, C., 'Antiquities from the River Blackwater III, Iron Axe-Heads' in *Ulster Journal of Archaeology*, 3rd series, 60 (2001), pp.63–93

Cannan, F., 'England's Irish Warriors' in *Military Illustrated*, no. 255 (Aug. 2009), pp.32–39.

Cannan, F., 'If the Father Hath Been a Galloglass…' in *Family History Monthly*, issue 180 (March 2010), pp.34–36

Cannan, F., 'Hags of Hell: Late Medieval Irish Kern' in *History Ireland*, volume 19, no. 1 (January/February 2011), pp.14–17

Cannan, F., 'A Family of Highland Blacksmiths: The Macnabs of Barachastlain' in *Journal of the Antique Metalware Society*, volume 19 (2011), pp.30–37

Cannan, F., 'Generation of Villains: Irish Kern' in *Military Illustrated*, no. 275 (April 2011), pp.24–31

Cannan, F., 'The "Clanranald Anvil"' in *Journal of the Antique Metalware Society*, volume 21 (2013), pp.50–57

Cannan, F., 'Holy Images from England: Medieval English Alabaster Sculpture in Ireland,' *History Ireland*, volume 22, no. 1 (Jan/Feb 2014), pp.16–18

Chahoud A. & Stagni, E., 'A Pseudo-Classical Dialogue in TCD MS 632' in *Hermathena*, no. 194 (summer 2013), pp.153–182

Cheape, H., 'Clanranald's Blacksmith' in *Clan Donald Magazine*, no. 12 (1991)

Chalmers, C. R. & Chaloner, E. J., '500 Years Later: Henry VIII, Leg Ulcers and the Course of History' in *Journal of the Royal Society of Medicine* (2009), pp.512–517

FitzGerald, W., 'The MacDonnells of Tinnakill Castle,' *Kildare Archaeological Society Journal*, 4 (1905), pp.205–215

Galofré-Vilà, G., Hinde, A. & Guntupalli, A. M., 'Heights Across the Last 2,000 Years in England' in *Research in Economic History*, 34 (2018), pp.67–98

Harbison, P., 'Native Irish Arms and Armour in Gaelic Literature, 1170–1600' in *The Irish Sword*, volume 12 (1975–1976), pp.173–199 & 270–284

Hayes-McCoy, G. A., 'The Gallóglach Axe' in *Journal of the Galway Archaeological and Historical Society*, 17 (1937), pp.101–121

Hore, H. F., 'Life in Old Ireland' in *Ulster Journal of Archaeology*, first series, volume 7 (1859), pp.267–277

Hore, H. F., 'The Rental Book of Gerald Fitzgerald, Ninth Earl of Kildare. Begun in the Year 1518,' *Journal of the Kilkenny and South-East of Ireland Archaeological Society*, new series, volume 2, no. 2 (1859), pp.266–280 & 301–310

McLynn, S., 'The Myths of Medieval Warfare' in *History Today*, volume 44, no. 1 (1994)

Morgan, M., 'Sunday 6 June 1518 – the Day the Renaissance Came to Ireland' in *History Ireland* (May/June 2012)

O'Neill, T., 'Edmund MacRichard Butler: Books and Warfare in Fifteenth-Century Ireland' in *History Ireland*, volume 23 (July/August 2015)

Smith, J. H., 'Letters Patent of James Mac Donnell' in *Ulster Journal of Archaeology*, 2 (1854), pp.121–125

Willis, T., 'A Two Handed Gaelic Irish Sword of the Sixteenth Century' in *The Fifteenth Park Lane Arms Fair* (1998), pp.18–27

Online Resource

CELT: The Corpus of Electronic Texts

Camden, William (D. F. Sutton ed.), *Britannia* (published online at the Philological Museum)

Cannan, F. 'Machiavellian Mercenaries? Galloglass Scruples of Politics, Culture & Religion' (published on Helion website, 2025)

Dictionary of Irish Biography

Dúchas.ie

Foras na Gaeilge's New English-Irish Dictionary

Harbison, P., 'An Illustration of the Lost Walsh Knight from the Jerpoint Cloister Arcade' (published on the website of the Kilkenny Archaeological Society)

History of Parliament Online

MacCarthy-Morrogh, M., 'The Munster Plantation, 1583–1641' Royal Holloway PhD thesis, 1983 (published on Royal Holloway College website)

Márkus, G, (trans. and ed.), *Adomnán's 'Law of the Innocents'* (Kilmartin House Trust, 2008; published online by eprints.gla.ac.uk)

Oxford Dictionary of National Biography

Oxford English Dictionary

Phelan, M. M., 'The Archedekins or MacCodys' (published on website of the Kilkenny Archaeological Society)

Purcell Horan, P., 'A Brief History of the Purcells of Ireland' (published on website of the Purcell Society)

Sherlock, R., 'Report on 'The Halberdier Wall Painting" (Archaeological Survey for Enniscorthy Castle, available on the Castle's website)

Also websites of British Museum, National Library of Ireland, Oxford University, Royal Collection & Trinity College Dublin library

About the author

Descended from Jacobites, redshanks and the medieval kings of Scotland, with a smattering of English men-at-arms, Fergus Cannan-Braniff's wide literary output includes the book *Galloglass 1250-1600* and works on medieval art and military history. Formerly of the Victoria & Albert Museum, he was Head of Religion & Philosophy at The Skinners' School, Kent, and recently appeared on History Hit discussing galloglass. He runs the living history group the Greensand Rangers, making much of his own kit.

About the artist

Seán Ó'Brógáin is based in Donegal, Ireland. He studied scientific and natural history illustration at Lancaster University and works for a wide range of international clients. His previous artwork for Helion has been included in *St Ruth's Fatal Gamble: The Battle of Aughrim 1691* and *the Fall of Jacobite Ireland*, *The King's Irish: The Royalist Anglo-Irish Foot of the English Civil War* and *The Men of Warre: The Clothes, Weapons and Accoutrements of the Scots at War 1460–1600*.

Other titles in the A Time of Knights series:

No 1 *Fall of the Merchant-Farmer Republic*
      The Battle of Visby 1361 and the Danish Conquest of Gotland
      Michael Fredholm von Essen

No 2 *The Scroll of Obadiah*
      The Life of a Norman Convert to Judaism in the First Crusade
      Frank Riess

No 3 *Birth of the Byzantine Army 476-641 CE*
      Volume 1: Still Late Roman?
      Philippe Richardot

No 4 *Birth of the Byzantine Army 476-641 CE*
      Volume 2: Watch them Fight!
      Philippe Richardot

No 5 *The Gaelic World at War*
      Soldiers & Soldiering in Ireland 1366-1547
      Fergus Cannan-Braniff